a Deeper Way

Deepen Your Journey *with* God

\- An Interactive Devotional -

Produced in the United States of America Published by Soul-Care Press Inc.

Soul-Care Press Inc.
Santa Cruz, California
Soul-Care.com

Cover Design: Soul-Care Press
Content, Developmental Editor & Co-Creator: Keri Lippman
Poetry: All poems by David Michael Lippman unless otherwise noted
Visit DavidMichaelLippman.Substack.com for more poetry

Original Package Design: Soul-Care Press Inc.

First Edition

10 9 8 7 6 5 4 3 2

Praise for *A Deeper Way*

"Most devotionals feel like something you should do. A Deeper Way is radically different. The color images and fresh ideas invite you into an experiential journey that brings clarity to your emotions, questions, and story. The pace is kind, the insights are hopeful, and the path is intentional."

"Like spending time at the ocean or in the clear mountain air, these pages offer refreshment for your heart, mind, and soul. Even better, it awakens an expectancy and hunger in you for the deeper, wilder, truer life God created you for."

Allen Arnold, *Executive Producer of Content, Wild at Heart & Author of The Story of With*

CONTENTS

Make sure to:

- Silence your phone
- Bring a journal & pen
- Grab a warm mug
- Find a quiet place
- Be kind to yourself

A Resource Unlike Any Other:

Longing. A familiar word that can make some of us ache and others of us filled with hope and anticipation. Often in our walks with Jesus, in the busyness of life, we may long for intentional time in God's presence and yet continue to find a variety of things hindering this intention. This sort of longing is from the Holy Spirit, but often it can be so hard to know how, or even where, to begin.

Some of us may have been waylaid or lost in disappointment, fear, or distraction. Still, that hunger for *more* remains. No matter where you are with God, this dynamic, interactive devotional has been created to enrich your times with the Lord.

Dynamic means that it is going to stir parts of your heart and mind that need to be awakened. *Interactive* means this devo creates unique moments for you and the Lord to engage in your two-way relationship. The more you lean in, the more you'll receive from this.

Think of this devo as a safe place. A place where you can process your internal world externally. A place where you can be guided through questions that can help not only guide you through the expected and anticipated, but unlock pieces of your heart that may be undiscovered or in need of healing.

Every question, every prompt, every interactive element is here to lead you closer to the One who made you for an intimate relationship with Himself.

This is your invitation to be still, pray, consider, and engage with whatever you might need during this time to respond to the gentle guidance of the Holy Spirit, carrying you into deeper union with the Father.

Because of Jesus Christ, we can approach God with confidence and explore the most honest, vulnerable, and needy parts of our hearts (Heb. 4:16, 10:19-25). So, spend some time *in the experience* of each section.

As you hold this guide, imagine yourself beginning a journey. But instead of planning the route ahead of time or stressing to think through all the details yourself, remember, you have a surprise Companion on this road who is here to meet with you, has already gone before you, and prepared all that you need!

This Companion is the Holy Spirit, the personal Presence of God, who is present within you and all around you. He is specifically present in the hearts of believers to lead each of His beloved ones into Truth.

Truth, in this case, can be the Truth and promises of Scripture, while also the truths of your heart as it grows and develops in relationship with God over your lifetime.

Consider as Father, Son, and Holy Spirit minister from a place of complete love and unity. Their love is infinite, grace is sufficient, light is pure and unshadowed, hope is potent, and all this is toward you and for you.

Like the Scriptures say, *the Spirit of Him who raised Christ from the dead lives in you, He…will also give life to your mortal bodies through His Spirit who dwells in you* (Rom 8:11).

Be prepared for Him to take you down roads of thought, feeling, or memory that may feel exciting at times, and also unfamiliar or stretching, for it is He that is at work in you, to will and work for His good pleasure. May this be a helpful expectation, granting faith to move into new frontiers in your relationship with Him.

So, listen to the moment. Take one sentence, one page, or one entry at a time. There are no page numbers in order for completion not to be a distraction or a goal.

Be drawn in, pause, breathe, ponder. Follow as you feel led.

Listen. Let your mind unravel. Think honestly.

Write. Draw. Doodle. Speak out loud.

Lament. Experience your heart.

Let the Life of God, the Holy Spirit, move the uncomfortable or unfamiliar or undiscovered parts of your heart toward His peace, life, and healing.

He has promised you abundance in relationship with Him.

Find it here.

Be Mindful:

- *This devo is interactive, so be ready to explore,* be creative, spontaneous, and surprised about how God leads and what surfaces as you explore. If you take one minute on one page, ten minutes on the next, and a week on another…that's what this is meant for!

- *When you're prompted to pause, consider, pray, etc., take a moment to actually do so.* Rather than simply trying to complete it in a timely manner, the content is designed to help you slow down, rest, and refresh with God. That may mean posturing your body and mind toward Him first before you feel it or experience the fruit in your heart. Progression is spending time with Jesus where He is leading, instead of simply completing the content.

- *You're invited not just to observe the landscape of your life, but to explore the hills and valleys with God who is already present there to meet you.* For the very trails that run through your heart and history are familiar roads for God, He has already been there, performed that powerful work of saving you, and wants to continue this gentle work until it is finished.

- *One question can often lead to a deeper question or even more content in your heart and life experience than you anticipated.* Truly, pray for the Lord to nudge your heart during the content to pause so you hear His invitation to dialogue in prayer. Often where your emotions are, where your mind resides or even wanders to the tasks of the day, is the very context where He wants to meet us. It's not just in our ideals or even places that seem good to go, but right where you are at, what you are feeling, what is being stirred.

- *There are journaling pages at intentional moments as invitations to be still and reflect.* Utilize these pages in conjunction with the content to integrate your heart and God's character. But of course, feel free to use your own journal instead and let the "journaling pages" be a clue to take an additional moment with the Lord to explore what's coming up for you.

- *As a Christian, we presume that, whether you know it or not, the Holy Spirit is already operating at a deep level in your life.* The hope is that these pages can help uncover His already active work in your life. So be open. Trust His promptings. Anticipate His guidance in the pages ahead.

- *Growth occurs in the journey between the reality of where you're at now and what God has said in His Word.* If we can see where we are and where we want to be, then we can clarify what sort of journey we're on. The images, prompts, and Scriptures throughout will help you notice the realities you are facing as well as the ideals of God's Word. As you see this reality, you can pay attention to God's active work there, and begin to take steps forward.

- *If and when negative feelings, resistance, or undesirable thoughts arise--notice those, be honest, and let those lead to conversation with God.* Rather than judging these reactions yourself, simply notice as they arise. Consider what you think of them. Then, ask God what He thinks of them. Allow the moment you notice distractions and disruption to be a prompt to reengage with His love. Often feelings of resistance are inlets toward deeper healing...

- *Ask God, what's going on in this? What's underneath my resistance?* They may be coming up because He is hoping you would bring them to Him. He isn't surprised, even if you are. If you get stuck, talk to God about what that experience is like for you being stuck. Every aspect of this journey can become part of your conversation with God.

- *If the trail feels oh too familiar, like a route you have traversed over and over in the same area* of pain, weakness, sin, brokenness, etc., then may you imagine a spiral staircase, that though the terrain seems to lead around the circle once again, consider the nuances, how it is unique this time, and what sort of new textures of thought or emotion you experience. This very well may be a new season, a different perspective, another layer of healing, a God-crafted insight, or a refreshed place of receiving. It may be that a fresh encounter is right around the corner.

- *Invite others into this journey with the Lord.* If you're experiencing anything from resistance and dryness to wonder and breakthrough...bring someone into the journey with you. When you speak your journey out loud, there is so much more to harvest. When you share it with someone who is a trusted friend, counselor, spiritual director, pastor, etc., then the questions and insights are even deeper. When you continue this journey with an individual or group, the conversation of growth can shape your community and culture and become contagious to those around you.

Be Expectant:

This interactive devo will help you to...

- Clarify your heart and, with the Lord, narrate the journey you find yourself on in this season.

- Acquire new insights, connections, and wisdom about your soul, your heart, your mind, and the layers that make you, you.

- Learn simple, yet powerful and profound ways to connect those areas with God in each section.

- Gather and Synthesize these learnings and insights at the end of each section as well as the end of the devo, cultivating a treasure chest of your interactions and discoveries from time with God, plus...

- In the end, you'll find an opportunity for all your content and reflection to come together into a structured experience for you to "Linger Longer" in your relationship with Him (*see Appendix*).

What would it look like to posture yourself with trust in the experiences ahead, to be expectant that our Good Guide will do beyond all that you ask or imagine according to His power already at work in you as you begin?

We bless you in this journey.

begin
the
journey

REST A
PALM

on your

chest

TAKE

A

deep

breath

wandering home

i have found a home
in love's low hills
you'd never notice me,
as you traced over their golden backs.
the waves of reeds sing
quietly muttering "today" and "now,"

and i do not worry about it,
you know, all those dirty things
our minds play games with
while we're gone,

no, i am no harlot here,
my home is the earth,
under the sun,
in the dirt,
away from all.

and you are invited
to our home of listening and waiting,
to meet in the great silent song
and rest.

do i sing here?
yes.

- INTRO -

GOD'S STORY & MY STORY

REHEARSE THE STORY

REMEMBER *His*-story and *your* story

Creation
God spoke the world into being - Genesis 1

Separation
Humanity chose to live apart from God - Genesis 3

Reconciliation
God chose to forgive Humanity through the sacrifice and resurection of Jesus - Romans 1-8

Restoration
God is restoring all things through the work of His Holy Spirit in the life of the Church and individuals - Colossians

We participate in God's story
As we spend time with Him...

THE BEGINNING

How Does His-story Intersect with Mine?

Creation - God made me

Birthday:__________ Parents:________________

What were the circumstances?

**if you don't know, ask someone who does!*

____
____
____
____

What's one thing someone loved about you as a kid?

**if you don't know, ask someone who does!*

____
____
____

Pray: *"God, thank You for making my life and writing every one of my days in Your book before I even existed. I am beloved because I am Yours." - Psalm 139:13-18*

THE LOSS

How Does His-story Intersect with Mine?

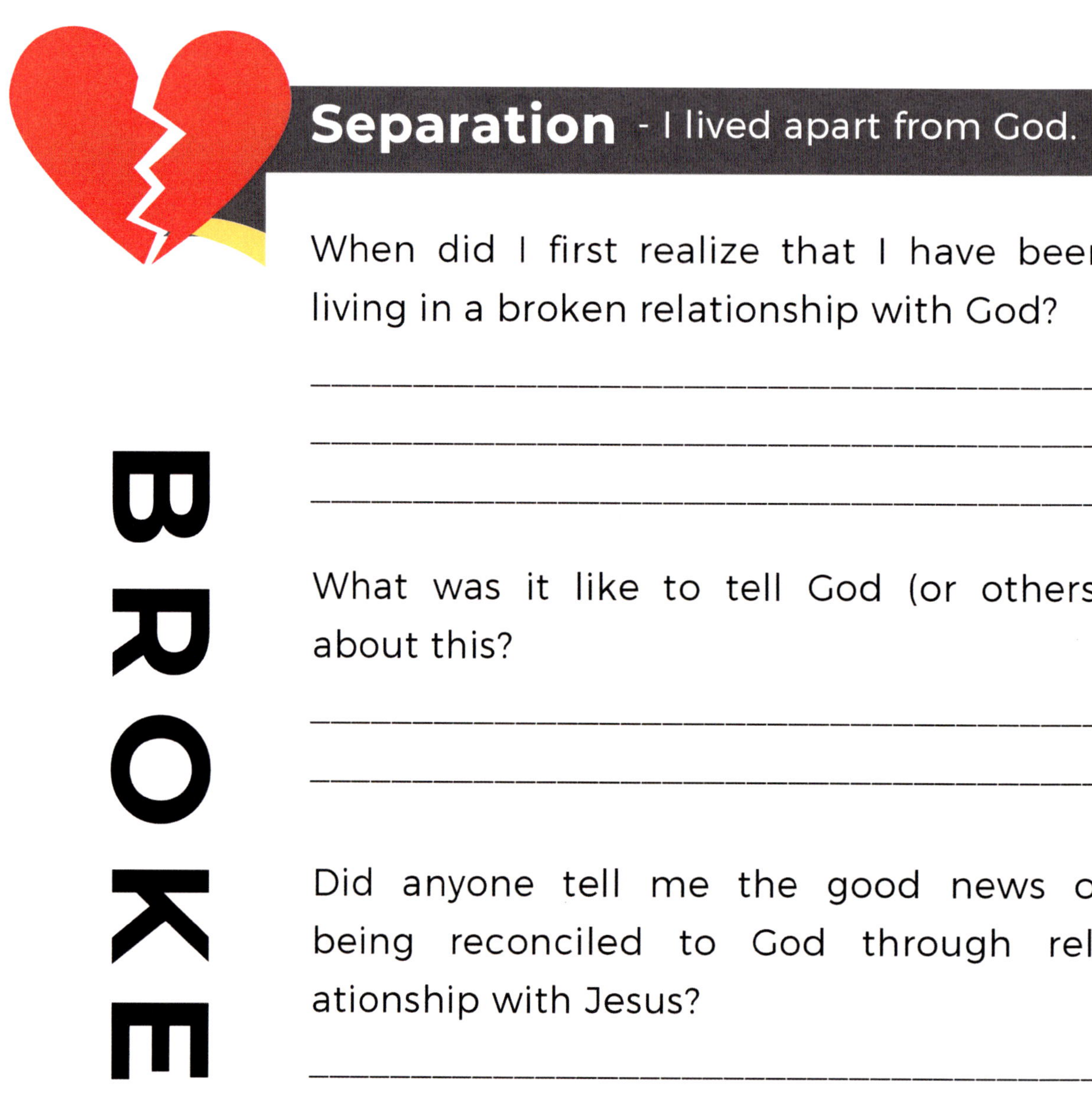

Separation - I lived apart from God.

When did I first realize that I have been living in a broken relationship with God?

____
____
____

What was it like to tell God (or others) about this?

____
____

Did anyone tell me the good news of being reconciled to God through relationship with Jesus?

____

Pray: *"God, I know I have sinned against You and others, but You have chosen me despite these offenses because of my faith in Jesus. Heal and transform my areas of brokenness, that I may know you in my deepest places."*

BROKEN

THE LOVE

How Does His-story Intersect with Mine?

What did Jesus do for me through His obedient life, death, and resurrection?

____

____

____

What was it like to receive the full forgiveness and acceptance of God's love?

____

____

What might be hindering me from walking in confidence with God in this season?____

____

Pray: "*God, You have brought me close through Your Son, Jesus, and now I can call myself a child of God. Would You help me know how to walk closer with You? I long to walk in the fullness of what You've done for me.*

BLESSED

THE NEW

How Does His-story Intersect with Mine?

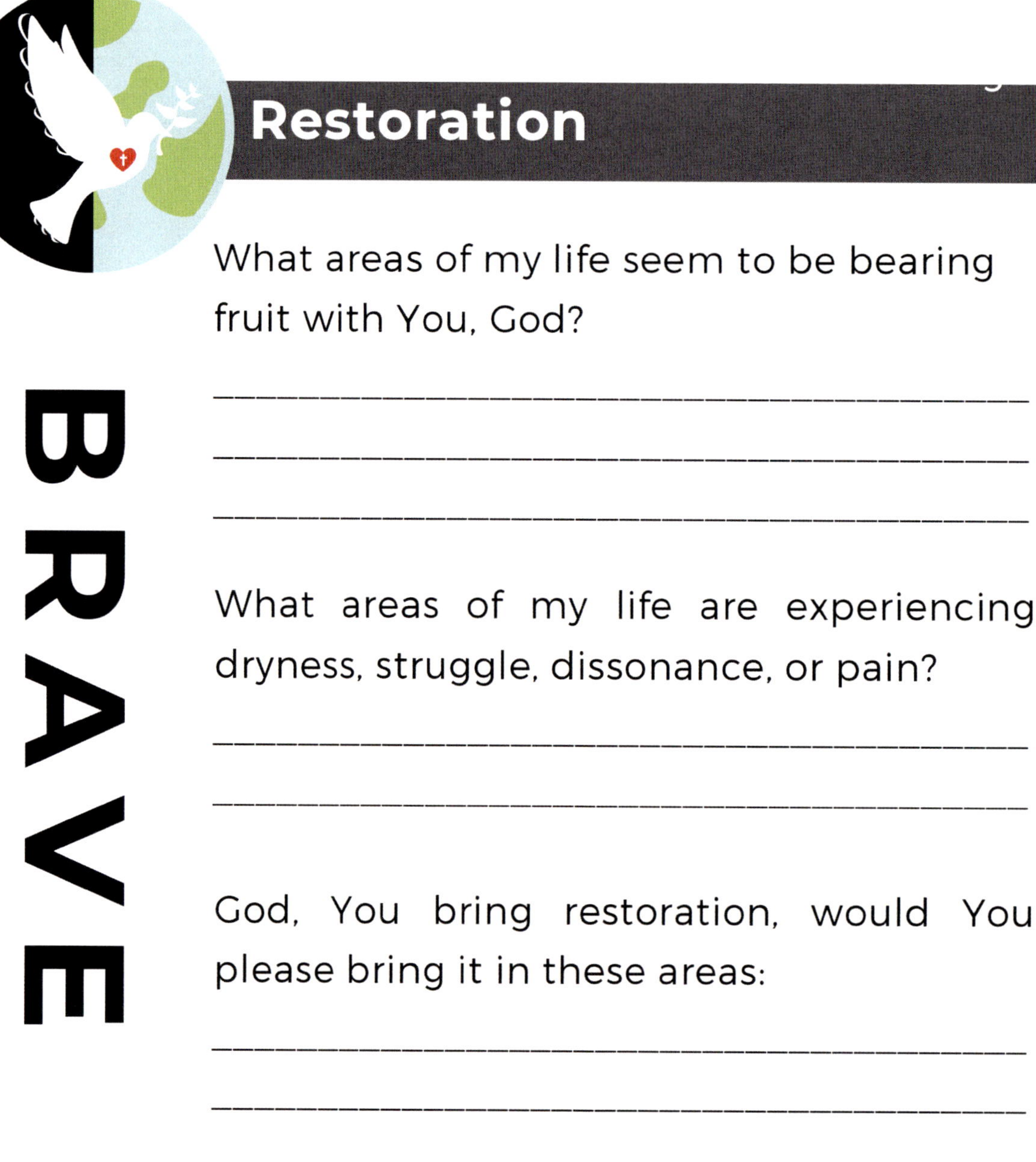

Restoration

What areas of my life seem to be bearing fruit with You, God?

____
____

____

What areas of my life are experiencing dryness, struggle, dissonance, or pain?

____

____

God, You bring restoration, would You please bring it in these areas:

____

____

Pray: *"God, You reign over every area of my life, the ones I am proud of, and the areas I am most ashamed of. Would You come with Your Holy Spirit and use our time together to bring restoration to every area of my walk with You."*

RESTORATION

Where have I found restoration?
(draw line from the world to an icon in the yellow section)

Where do I still need restoration?
(draw a line from the dove to an icon in the grey section)

I WONDER...
What would it be like to talk with Jesus about these things?
Come to Me all you who are weary and burdened...
And I will give you rest.
MATTHEW 11:28

CONVERSATION

Let's begin exploring how to:

- **Talk Honestly with God in Prayer**

- **Bring Up Heart-Level Issues in Prayer**

- **Grow in Self- awareness and God-awareness**

- **Notice Spiritual Blind-spots & Hurdles**

- **Understand how God speaks to you**

- **Connect your story to God's story**

- **Trust His leadership For your life**

- **Create your own Personal retreat time**

God created you
to walk intimately with Him

BEGIN WITH PRAYER

"Dear God,

I have been longing to walk
Closer to You.

The Bible promises that You are *Good*
And that You're near to me.

Sometimes it's hard to hear Your
Voice because of '______________,'

But I still need You and ask for
the help of Your Holy Spirit

To protect my every thought
Encourage my heart

To guide me and be with me
Every step of the way...

Finish this prayer in your journal or in the space provided:
____
____
____

JOURNAL HERE

JOURNAL HERE

A DEEPER DIALOGUE

SOLITUDE IS THE FURNACE OF TRANSFORMATION. WITHOUT SOLITUDE WE REMAIN VICTIMS OF OUR SOCIETY

A DEEPER DIALOGUE:

The word solitude can at times both beckon and intimidate. It can feel full of longing while also feeling daunting. Some of us come hungry for "more" of God. Others come weary, wounded, or dry. What is it that we're wanting? And what are His desires for this time? How do we enter into this sacred space in such a way that we know we've met with God?

All these interior movements of mind and heart can become knotted as we draw near to the One who promises to draw near to us (James 4:8).

Discovering how to navigate this is the reason *A Deeper Way* was created.

Our souls are made to live and dwell in active relationship with God. But a thousand pressures and requirements can war against the rest our soul needs. How do we bring these lived realities to God without getting lost in the fog of distraction, fear, grief, or doubt?

This time of solitude will be a space to begin to see 1) the reality of our lives, 2) the reality of our hearts and 3) how that's shaped the way we see and relate to God. In this space, as we pray, our inner world can rise into our consciousness—this may feel uncomfortable and unfamiliar—but it is good. Why good?

God says He knows us inside and out (Psalm 139:1-6) and He wants us to share our honest heart process with Him (Isaiah 29:13). More so, the false images or impure intuitions we have of God and ourselves actually affect our communion with God. In The Pursuit of God, A.W. Tozer says, *"The most portentous fact about any man is not what he at a given time may say or do —but what he in his deep heart conceives God to be like...*

This time of solitude actually makes space for God to be with us like a friend, and say something like, "When that was happening, you may have experienced it this way. I see that. And I see *you.* I notice *this* about you."

Or, "Did you know where I was then? I want to show you." Or, "Wow, yeah that was really hard, can we process talk through what happened together?"

"CHRISTIANITY WITHOUT REAL EXPERIENCE OF GOD WILL EVENTUALLY BE NO CHRISTIANITY AT ALL."

- TIM KELLER

It is impossible to keep our moral practices sound and our inward attitudes right, while our idea of God is erroneous or inadequate.....We tend by a secret law of the soul, to move toward our mental image of God." It's as if our wounds and sins affect our picture of God, and draw our hearts away from the accurate reality of His love.

Since our goal in solitude is to share personal connection with God, we are invited to be open to see anything in the way, to notice what has been, and what's shaped us, and, as best we can, to speak authentically with God. And in this way, we engage in His already active work. For He's been part of our process the whole time.

The goal of this section is to facilitate your time of solitude to intentionally reflect and open to this conversation with the Lord, in order to receive from Him the care you need.

These questions and content are a tool for discerning the state of your soul before God. Your answers will narrow your focus and clarify your heart and longings. Be honest.

Remember, these questions are for you! Knowing your heart will deepen your conversations with God and shed light on His leadership. Even now, you're taking the first steps toward this time in His love...

SHARE WITH GOD

God, my times alone with You have been...

(circle one)

lonely

anxious

boring   routine

silent

peaceful

desperate

other:__________

delightful

insightful

needed

confusing

awesome

sporadic   dry

God, what I long for in time with you is...

(circle one)

connection   comfort   healing

strength   answers   restoration   truth

calm

peace   assurance

other:__________

favor   knowledge   love

Take a moment now and share these
thoughts with God...

GOD'S PRESENCE

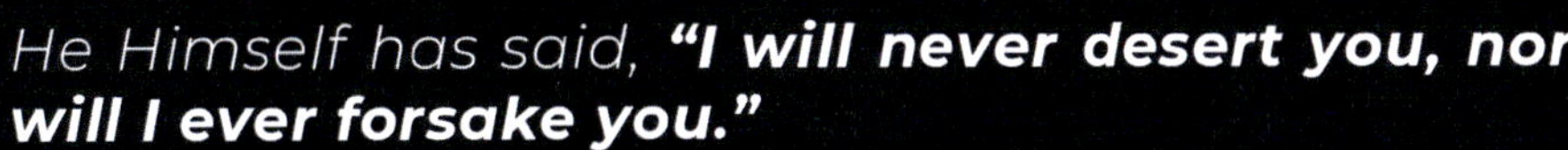

He Himself has said, **"I will never desert you, nor will I ever forsake you."**

Hebrews 13:5

"I will not leave you as orphans; I will come to you."

John 14:18

He, your Teacher will no longer hide Himself, but **your eyes will behold your Teacher. Your ears will hear a word behind you, "This is the way, walk in it," whenever you turn to the right or to the left.**

Isaiah 30:20-21

Where can I go from Your Spirit? Or where can I flee from Your presence? If I ascend to heaven, You are there; If I make my bed in Hell, behold, You are there. If I take the wings of the dawn, if I dwell in the remotest part of the sea, even there Your hand will lead me, and Your right hand will lay hold of me. If I say, "Surely the darkness will hide me, and the light around me will be night," **Even the darkness is not dark to You, and the night is as bright as the day. Darkness and light are alike to You.**

Psalm 139:7-12

"When you pass through the waters, I will be with you; and through the rivers, they will not overflow you. When you walk through the fire, you will not be scorched, nor will the flame burn you. "For I am the Lord your God, the Holy One of Israel, your Savior... **"Since you are precious in My sight, since you are honored and I love you...do not fear, for I am with you."**

Isaiah 43:4-6

JOURNAL HERE

NOTICING THE JOURNEY

What comes up when you're alone...

(with God)

Drawn toward deeper

Let's look at what is inside of that desire to be with God...

Begin to notice...

Attune to His voice...

Learn how to be present *with* the One who is always present to you...

dialogue with God...

The IDEAL
What are your hopes and expectations?

NOTICING THE JOURNEY

What comes up when you're alone...

The IDEAL

I will run in the path of your commandments... When you enlarge my heart!

Psalm 119:32

As you read this, what stands out to you?

JOURNAL HERE

NOTICING THE JOURNEY

What comes up when you're alone...

The REAL

O people, pour out your heart before him; God is a refuge for us.

Psalm 62:8

Casting all your anxieties on him... he cares for you.

1 Peter 5:7

As you read this, what stands out to you?

I will sprinkle clean water on you, and you will be clean; I will cleanse you... from all your idols. Moreover, I will give you a new heart and put a new spirit within you; I will and remove the heart of stone from your flesh and give you a heart of flesh. I will put My Spirit within you and cause you to walk in My statutes.

Ezekiel 36:25-27

To remain present to God you must remain present to your heart

John Eldredge *Waking the Dead*

JOURNAL HERE

NOTICING THE JOURNEY

What comes up when you're alone...

HOLDING REAL & IDEAL

Holding the Real & Ideal before God

Open before you all that you've noticed. Let God's light shine on these things...

Let Him see the IDEALS you're drawn toward...

Let Him hold the REAL you're living in...

Hold BOTH before Him, just be OPEN. Begin to notice and to talk with Him about what you see...

JOURNAL HERE

HOLDING REAL & IDEAL

Holding the Real & Ideal before God

as you pause with God...

"Be filled with the Holy Spirit."

Eph 5:18

NOTICING THE JOURNEY

Holding the Real & Ideal before God

The JOURNEY

You *and*
Holy Spirit

Now, what words would you use to describe your journey?

-
-
-
-
-
-

- Ex: Long, exciting, arduous, steep, momentous, epic, dangerous, wonderful, etc.

A Navigator's Notes:

The IDEAL - God gave this to you, in His Word, in your desires, remember You are not going to get there in your own strength, and His ideas of this may look different than yours.

The REAL - The Holy Spirit dwells in the reality of our hearts and minds, with us, (Rom 8:26) , and He will only let us begin from where we are.

The JOURNEY - Where are you now? Where is God's Presence? What limitations are you experiencing? Any initial responses? Offer these to God.

Be Kind to yourself - Allow the Holy Spirit to minister to you where you're at and pace yourself with Him. Allow Him to nuance in prayerful reflection the REAL and the IDEAL to His ways and heart for you.

JOURNAL HERE

WHO AM I ENCOUNTERING?

Myself
"That you may prosper...
As your soul prospers."
3 John 1:2

the enemy
"He stood before God
accusing them
day and night."
Revelation 12:10

Jesus
"This is My Beloved Son,
listen to Him."
Mark 9:7

other

Often times we don't know right away
in the quiet if it's the enemy, ourselves, or
the voice of Jesus...

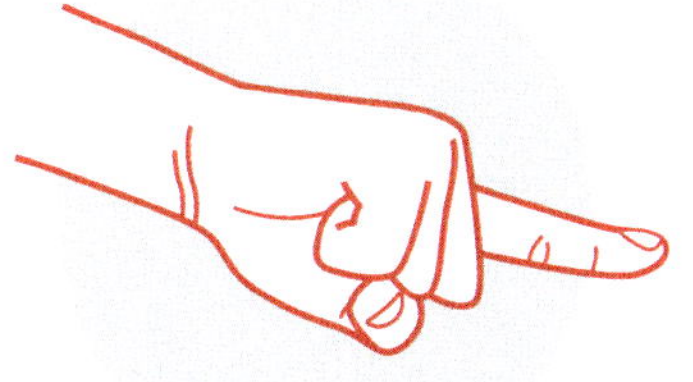

the enemy

"he stood before God accusing them day and night."
Revelation 12:10

What does the enemy sound like?

When I hear that voice, I'm going to...

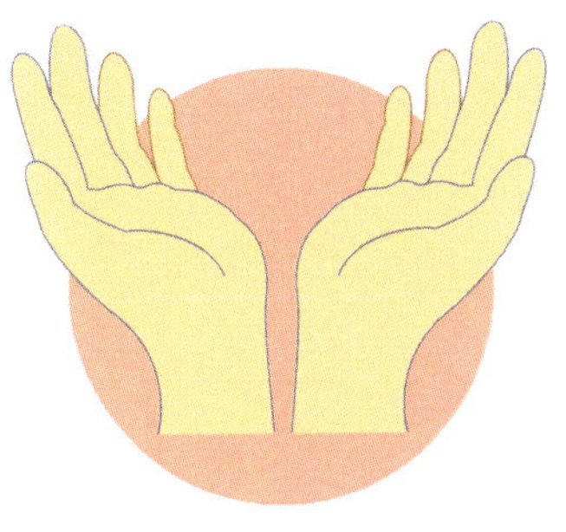

Myself

"That you may prosper... As your soul prospers."
3 John 1:2

What does my voice sound like?

When I hear that voice, I'm going to...

Jesus

"This is My Beloved Son, listen to Him."
Mark 9:7

What does Jesus's voice sound like?

When I hear that voice, I'm going to...

But as we offer this time to God, we can entrust the journey to Him...

Submit yourselves therefore to God.

Resist the devil, and he will flee from you.

Draw near to God, and He will draw near to you.

Cleanse your hands...and purify your hearts...

James 4:7-8

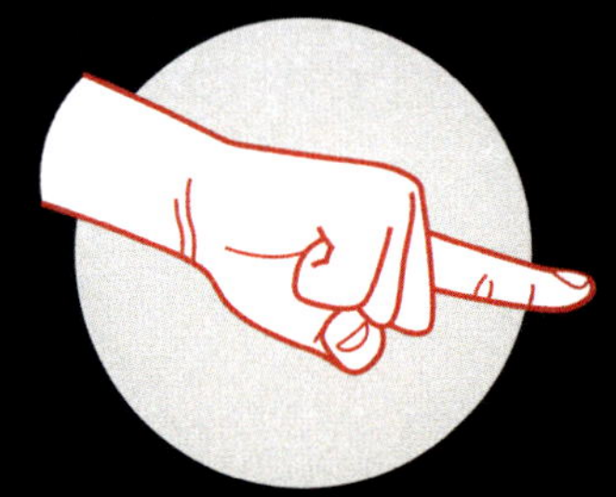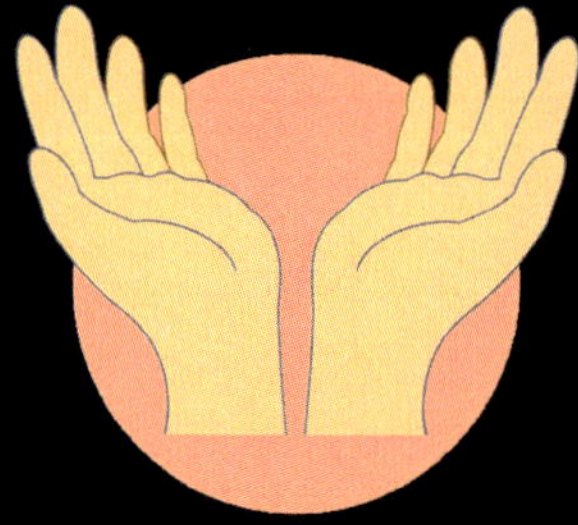

JOURNAL HERE

Take a moment to pray and stand on God's Word and ask His Spirit to lead

"Solid food is for the mature, for those who have their powers of discernment trained by constant practice to distinguish good from evil."

Hebrews 5:14

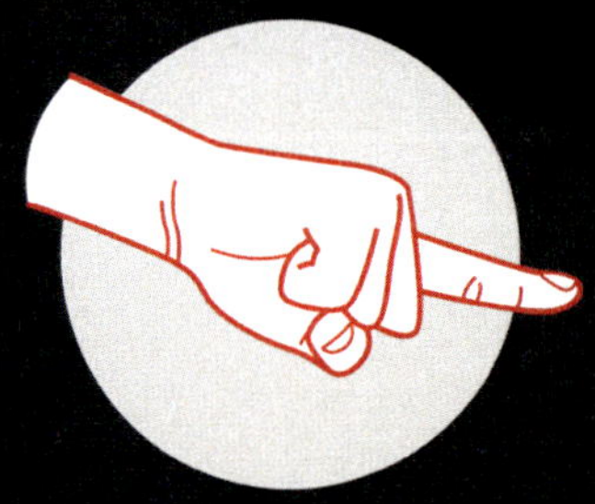 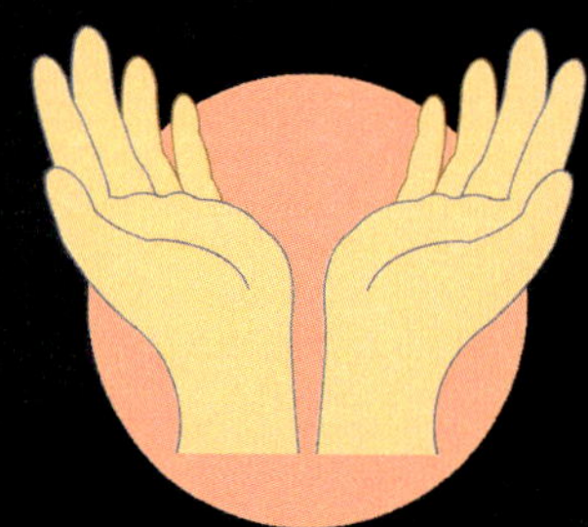 

JOURNAL HERE

I arise today through a mighty strength, the invocation of the Trinity,

Through belief in the Threeness, through confession of the Oneness

of the Creator of creation.

I arise today through the strength of Christ's birth with His baptism,

Through the strength of His crucifixion with his burial,

Through the strength of His

resurrection with His ascension,

Through the strength of His

descent for the judgment of doom.

I arise today, through

God's strength to pilot me,

God's might to uphold me,

God's wisdom to guide me,

God's eye to look before me,

God's ear to hear me,

God's word to speak for me,

God's hand to guard me,

God's shield to protect me,

God's host to save me

From snares of devils,

From temptation of vices,

From everyone who shall wish me ill,

afar and near.

I summon today

All these powers between me and those evils,

Against every cruel and merciless power

that may oppose my body and soul,

Christ with me,

Christ before me,

Christ behind me,

Christ in me,

Christ beneath me,

Christ above me,

Christ on my right,

Christ on my left,

Christ when I lie down,

Christ when I sit down,

Christ when I arise,

Christ in the heart of every

man who thinks of me,

Christ in the mouth of

everyone who speaks of me,

Christ in every eye that sees me,

Christ in every ear that hears me.

A Prayer of Protection - St. Patrick's Breastplate

FOLLOWING JESUS

"Very early in the morning, while it was still dark, Jesus got up, left the house and went off to a solitary place, where he prayed." (Mark 1:35)

"When Jesus heard [that John the Baptist had been beheaded], he withdrew by boat privately to a solitary place." (Mt 14:13)

"The news about him spread all the more... but Jesus often withdrew to lonely places and prayed." (Luke 5:15-16)

"After [Jesus] had dismissed [the crowds], he went up on a mountainside by himself to pray. When evening came, he was [still] there alone." (Matthew 14:23)

"Jesus went out to a mountain side to pray, and spent the night praying to God. When morning came, he called his disciples to him." (Luke 6:12-13)

[Jesus] said to [his disciples], 'Come with me by yourselves to a quiet place and get some rest.' So they went away by themselves in a boat to a solitary place." (Mark 6:31-32)

Just as Jesus leaned on the Father
So in our solitude, we too, can lean on Him.

i took the first steps into my room during a silent retreat in big sur, ca. it'd been awhile since i'd gone away just to be with jesus. i needed it.

the room was simple, and the view was gorgeous. a sliding glass door opened to a private view of the pacific ocean. wow, marvelous. my spirit began to breathe. my shoulders relaxed. i slipped my sandals off and put my things on the floor.

i leaned on the wall
and opened my hands.
to let go of the day-to-day.
to begin to let my soul out of its cage.

even as i write this i can remember. and it stills my soul. the smell of the sea. the warm air. the sunlight on oak trees. i was drawn into rest. the expanse of the ocean became a canvas for god's handiwork. my room became holy ground. sacred space for me and jesus to meet. lyrics leapt out of my pen and into my journal, moments of quiet captured forever...

THIS SEASON:

What about your current season of life has led you to desire this deeper conver-sation with God?

What are some of the
questions or conflicts
contained within those
circumstances in this
season of life?

*Write a list or draw
an image of this
season, then jot a
sentence in the box
about what it now
contains.*

In those circum-
stances and conflicts
what would be the
desired or best
result?

*Draw a picture (or write a list) of the **worst** possibilities that could happen in this current circumstance.*

Talk to God about the **best** and the **worst** for a moment. Then, write a note about that interaction:

CONSIDER

List a similar situation(s) you've been through
comparable to those above.

Situation #1

Similarities?

Situation #2

THE FIRST SITUATION
ponder situation #1

What was good in
that situation?

What was hard in
that situation?

What would you
like to repeat again?

What would you
never want to
repeat?

**What could've made
that season easier?**

**What increased the
difficulty of that time?**

JOURNAL HERE

THE SECOND SITUATION
ponder situation #2

What was good in
that situation?

What was hard in
that situation?

What would you
like to repeat again?

What would you
never want to
repeat?

**What could've made
that season easier?**

**What increased the
difficulty of that time?**

LASTLY, LET'S CONSIDER

Overlapping similarities in these circumstances:

What do those similarities imply about God? Be honest.

____

Be as honest as possible!

Similarities?

What do those similarities imply about who you are?

____

Be as honest as possible!

love's shadow

logs crackle in flame.
i breathe soot in out as
steam wisps like a ghost i sip.

love is such a face that has grown
unfamiliar over the years,
oh it has come close,
but it's just as blurred.
i can't make it out.
so still i go and stay
i play the game,

but love is like shadow,
coming close,
just beyond my eyes,
a form i can't make out
and well i see it
and oh i feel it
but can i know it
does it see me here?

MY TIME WITH GOD

How did my experience in those situations affect my time with God?

"Without knowledge of God There is no knowledge of self

- JOHN CALVIN, *INSTITUTES*

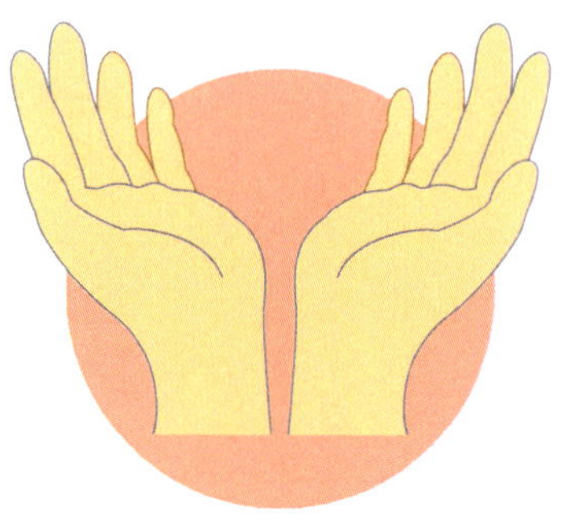

Without knowledge of self There is no knowledge of God"

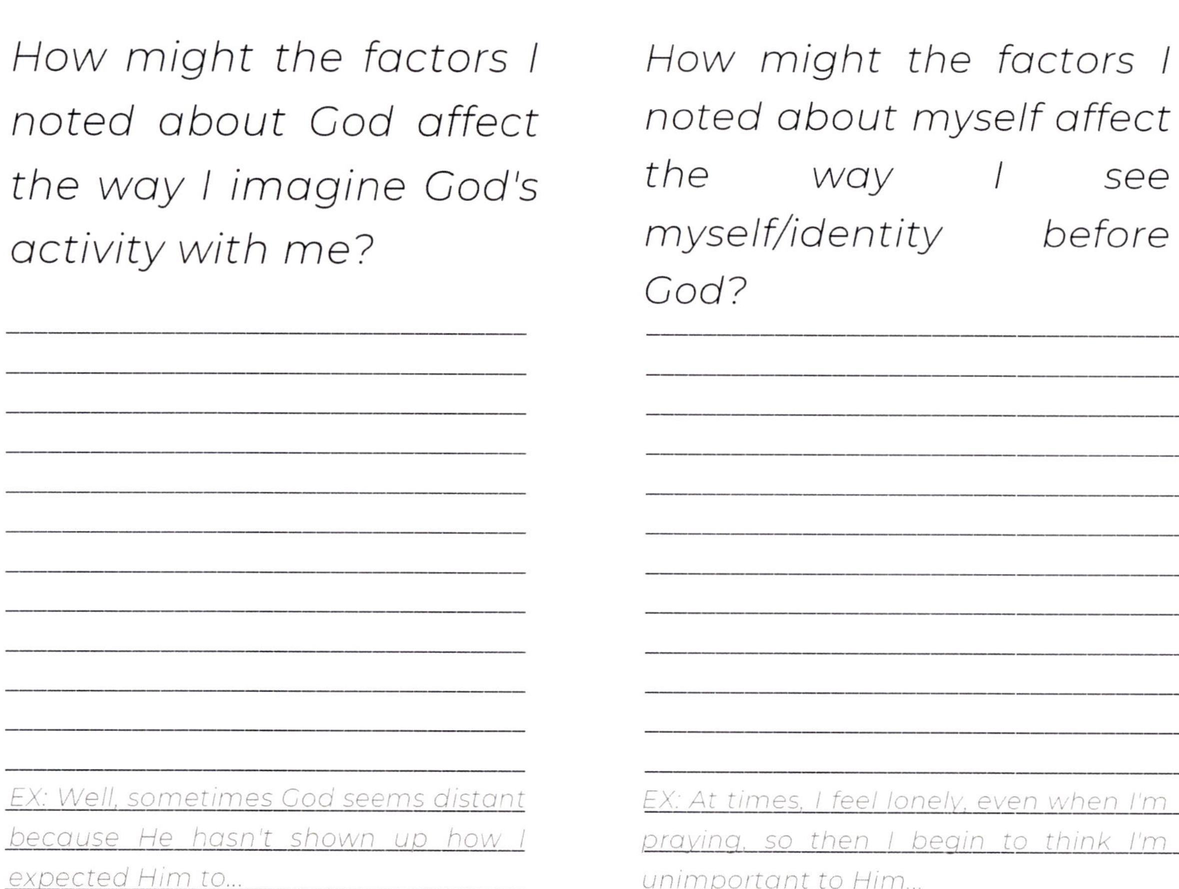

How might the factors I noted about God affect the way I imagine God's activity with me?

____
____
____
____
____
____
____
____
____
____
____

EX: Well, sometimes God seems distant because He hasn't shown up how I expected Him to...

How might the factors I noted about myself affect the way I see myself/identity before God?

____
____
____
____
____
____
____
____
____
____
____

EX: At times, I feel lonely, even when I'm praying, so then I begin to think I'm unimportant to Him...

TALK TO GOD ABOUT THIS:

Take a moment to listen...

What do you sense God might be saying to you?

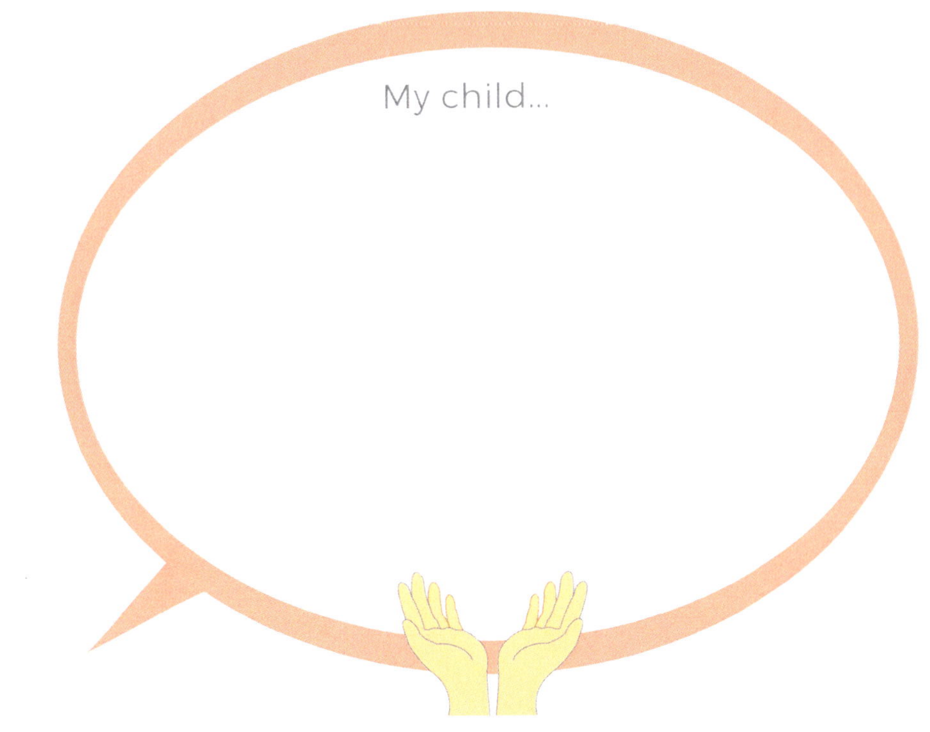

ANCIENT PRAYER

BY GEORGE HERBERT, 1633

Lord, who createdst man in wealth and store,
Though foolishly he lost the same,
Decaying more and more,
Till he became
Most poore:
With thee
O let me rise
As larks, harmoniously,
And sing this day thy victories:
Then shall the fall further the flight in me.

My tender age in sorrow did beginne
And still with sicknesses and shame.
Thou didst so punish sinne,
That I became
Most thinne.
With thee
Let me combine,
And feel thy victorie:
For, if I imp my wing on thine,
Affliction shall advance the flight in me.

JOURNAL HERE

WHILE LISTENING...

The purpose of this Christian life is that our hearts might be restored and set free.

JOHN ELDREDGE

SCRIPTURE

> He awakens me morning by morning, He awakens my ear
> to listen as a disciple, the Lord God has opened my ear.
>
> - ISAIAH 50:4-5

Take a breath.

Then read these Scriptures below.

Ask God to open your ears to His Holy Spirit,

Let the words wash over you once.

Then read it again.

Practice receiving these words as...

God's word to you.

SCRIPTURE

Psalm 62:5-8

Let all that I am
Wait quietly before God,
For my hope is in Him.
He alone is my rock
and my salvation,
My fortress where
I will not be shaken.
My victory
and honor
Come from
God alone.

He is my refuge, a rock
where no enemy can reach me.
O my people, trust in Him at all times.
Pour out your heart to Him,
For God is our refuge.

SCRIPTURE

Psalm 131:1-3

Lord, my heart is not proud;
My eyes are not haughty.
I don't concern myself
With matters too great
or too awesome
for me to grasp.

Instead,
I have calmed
And quieted myself,
Like a weaned child
Who no longer cries for
Its mother's milk. Yes, like a
weaned child is my soul within me.

O Israel, put your hope in the Lord—
Now and always.

REFLECTION

What did I learn about myself in this last section?

What did I learn about you, God, in this last section?

If someone were going through a similar season as me, I would share this with them:

- SECTION II -

DYNAMICS OF DESIRE

THE IMAGINATION OF MAN HAS [A FUNCTION & DUTY FROM THE FATHER]...THAT OF FOLLOWING AND FINDING OUT THE DIVINE IMAGINATION IN WHOSE IMAGE IT WAS MADE.

-GEORGE MACDONALD

DYNAMICS OF DESIRE:

What comes up when you think about desire? Being drawn toward a thing is a natural function of being human. We're drawn to physical things like food, fragrance, and touch. We're also drawn to spiritual things, like wonder, beauty, and deep ideas about the world.

Desires root themselves deep in us. Some begin early in our childhood, before memory. Others develop over years of habits in families, culture, churches, etc. Even deeper, desire itself is part of God's love that He wired into us. Desire itself is a gift. It is what brings us into meaningful connection with the world, each other, and God.

Yet, desire can confuse us, lead us astray, or overtake us in ways we don't ultimately want. There are layers of complexity here, but there is One who understand completely our desires, One who lived with powerful desires Himself, and One who seeks to dream with us and share desires.

Jesus reveals that God the Father loves us and means to do a powerful work within our desires. And since desires are central to relationship, it is at that level that God often works in order to bring us to Himself. He also works within our desire to pour out His love to others.

JOURNAL HERE

WHAT GOD DESIRES...

God **desires** all men to be **saved** and to **come to the knowledge** of the **truth**
1 Timothy 2:3-4

Father, I **desire** that they also, whom You have given me, **may be with Me** where I am, **to see My glory** that You have given Me.
John 17:24

Behold, You **desire truth in the innermost being**, And in the hidden part You will make me know **wisdom**.
Psalm 51:6

But go and learn what this means: 'I **desire compassion**, and **not sacrifice**,' for I did not come to call the righteous, but sinners."
Matthew 9:13

But go and learn what this means: 'I **desire compassion**, and **not sacrifice**,' for I did not come to call the righteous, but sinners."
Matthew 9:13

For **the Father Himself loves you,** because you have loved Me and have believed that I came forth from the Father.
John 16:27

Behold, **I will allure her**. Bring her into the wilderness and **speak kindly to her.** Then I will **give** her her vineyards from there, And the valley of [Trouble] as a door of **hope**. And she will sing there as in the days of her youth,
Hosea 2:14-15

Can a woman forget her nursing child and have no compassion on the son of her womb? Even these may forget, but **I will not forget you.** Behold, **I have inscribed you on the palms of My hands;** Your walls are continually before Me.
Isaiah 49:15-17

What other desires can you think of? Holiness? Peace? Reconciliation? Joy? Justice? Other ones?

Write down a few of God's desires that you noticed:

What comes up when
You think of God's desires?

What additional desires might God have?

What might it be like to share yours with Him too?

"Entering a private room and shutting the door....does not mean that we immediately shut out all our inner doubts, anxieities, fears, bad memories, unresolved conflicts, angry feelings and impulsive desires....

"When we have removed our outer distractions, we often find that our inner distractions manifest themselves to us in full force. We often use the outer distractions to shield ourselves from the interior noises. *This makes the discipline of solitude all the more important.*"

— HENRI NOUWEN
MAKING ALL THINGS NEW & OTHER CLASSICS

JOURNAL HERE

IN THE END THE HUMAN SOUL WILL CHOOSE WHAT IT MOST WANTS.

IF WE ARE BRAVE ENOUGH TO STAY WITH THIS EXPERIENCE OF WANTING SOMETHING WE DO NOT YET HAVE...

WE DISCOVER THAT UNDERNEATH ALL OTHER DESIRE IS A DESIRE FOR GOD, FOR LOVE, FOR THE TRUE BELONGING.

— RUTH HALEY BARTON,
INVITATION TO SILENCE & SOLITUDE

DISTRACTIONS?

Circle the areas that seem to lead your mind away from God...

relationships

work

desires

busyness

finances

ministry

pleasing others

fear

heaviness

other

What if these distractions became areas you could share with God?

What would you share with Him?

JOURNAL HERE

GOD, WHAT DO I WANT?

Our **desires** can teach us so much about where we're at currently and help us notice what God is doing, how He's drawing us to Himself.

While at the same time desire can mislead us from seeing the reality of our lives and become a feeling we chase instead of God Himself.

What do we do with desire?

JOURNAL HERE

GOD, WHAT DO I WANT?

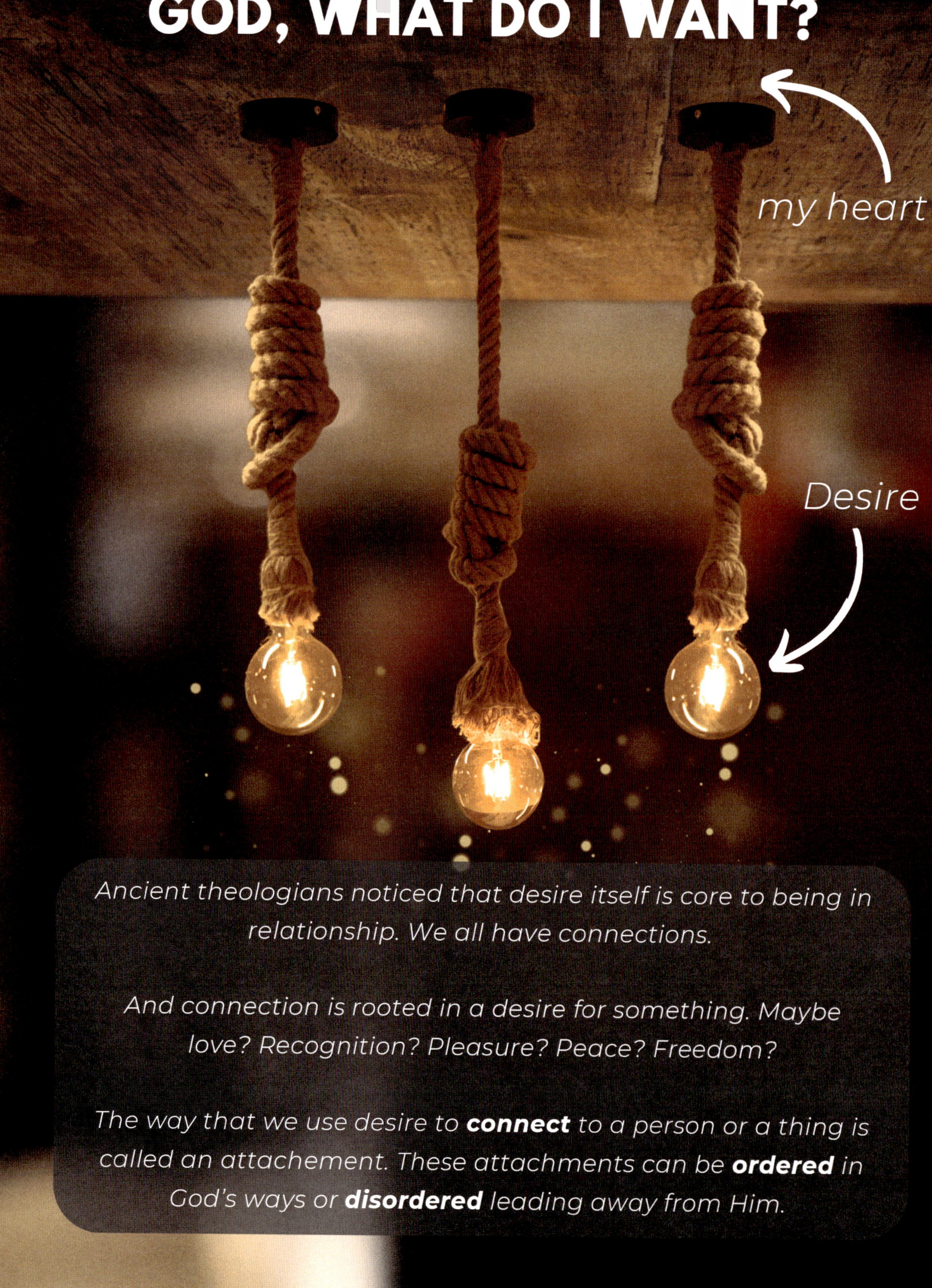

Ancient theologians noticed that desire itself is core to being in relationship. We all have connections.

And connection is rooted in a desire for something. Maybe love? Recognition? Pleasure? Peace? Freedom?

The way that we use desire to **connect** to a person or a thing is called an attachement. These attachments can be **ordered** in God's ways or **disordered** leading away from Him.

GOD, WHAT DO I WANT?

As we see the ordered attachment
or the disordered attachment
TO
a desire,
THEN
we can see our hearts and God's heart more clearly
AND
Discern the good within that **desire,** reconnect with God,
and adjust any disorder in HIs love…

JOURNAL HERE

WHAT DESIRES DO YOU NOTICE?

JOURNAL HERE

WHAT DESIRES DO YOU NOTICE?

my heart

a connection

These could be a...
Relationship
Career
Skill
Idea/Concept
Prayer
Wound
Dream
Other?

Desire

What is **good** in this desire?

What in this is **from God?**

Or leading me **to God?**

What is **good** in this desire?

What in this is **from God?**

Or leading me **to God?**

What is **good** in this desire?

What in this is **from God?**

Or leading me **to God?**

JOURNAL HERE

WHAT DESIRES DO YOU NOTICE?

JOURNAL HERE

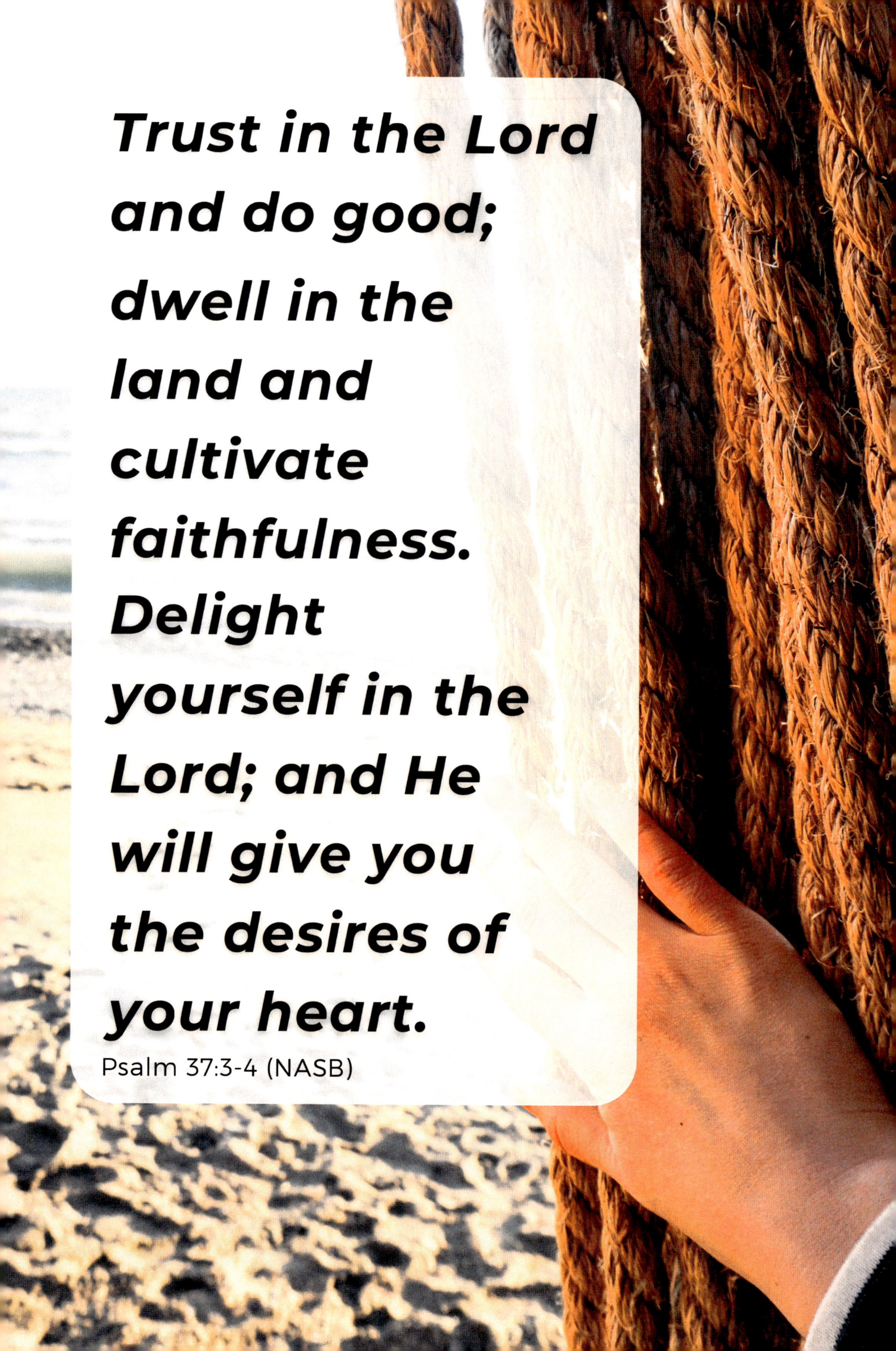
Trust in the Lord and do good; dwell in the land and cultivate faithfulness. Delight yourself in the Lord; and He will give you the desires of your heart.
Psalm 37:3-4 (NASB)

JOURNAL HERE

HOLDING DISAPPOINTMENT

Desire is God's idea

Unprocessed dis-appointment can sit in our hearts, and influence our desire...

It can affect what we choose, when we act, or what we imagine when we think of God and others...

And steal our ability to choose God's best...

- **What areas of disappointment are you carrying?**

- **When has this affected your connection to God?**

- **When has this affected your connection to others?**

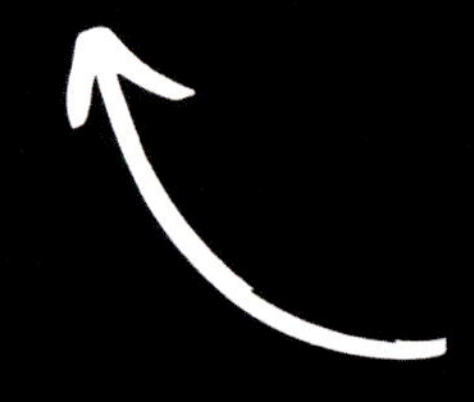

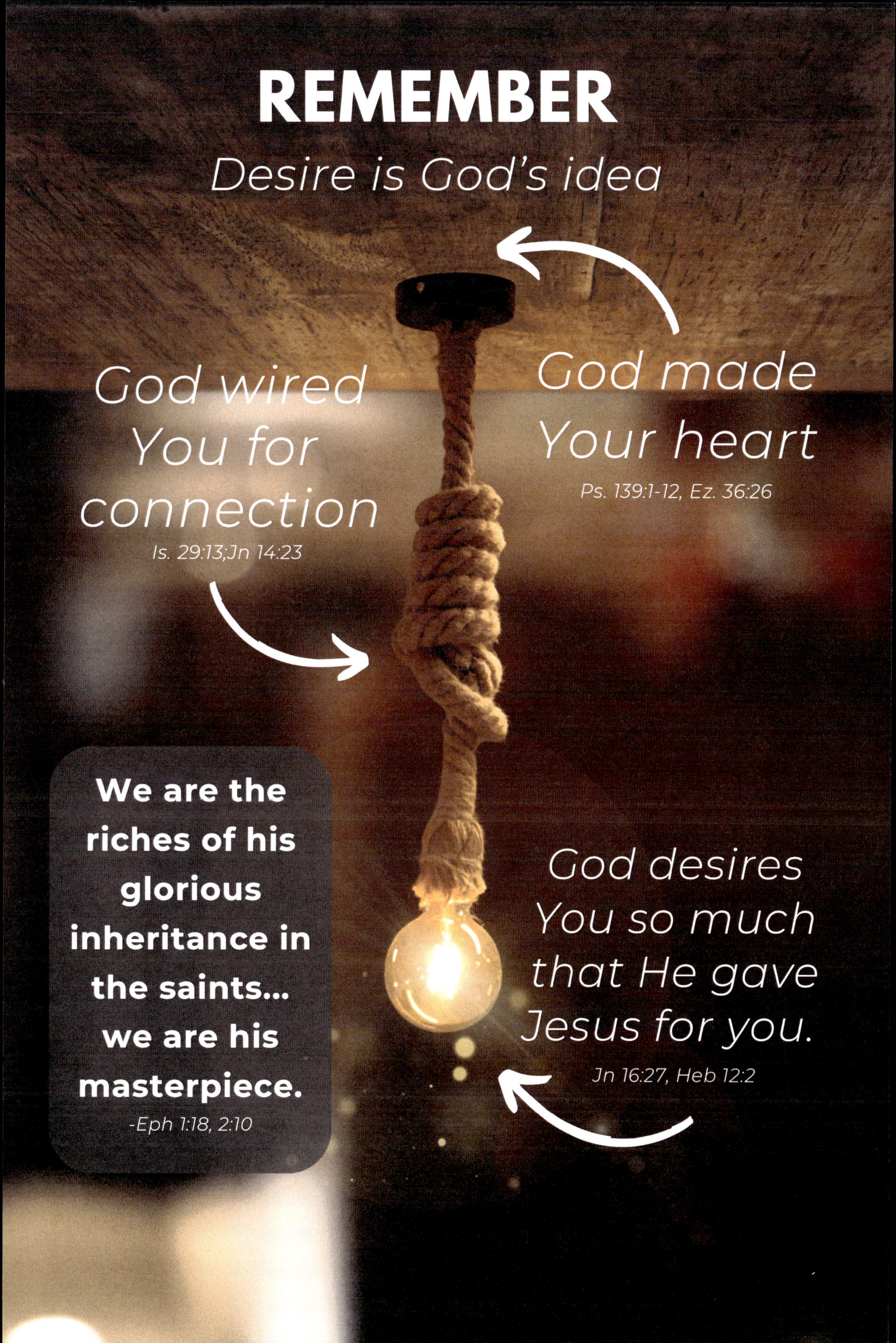

REMEMBER
Desire is God's idea

God made
Your heart
Ps. 139:1-12, Ez. 36:26

God wired
You for
connection
Is. 29:13;Jn 14:23

We are the
riches of his
glorious
inheritance in
the saints...
we are his
masterpiece.
-Eph 1:18, 2:10

God desires
You so much
that He gave
Jesus for you.
Jn 16:27, Heb 12:2

REMEMBER

Desire is God's idea

a God connection

What would it look like if this desire was connected to God?

What would it be like to attach to Him, in order to better attach to this area?

God's heart

What does your desire show you about God's heart?

What would it be like to offer this area to Him to grow together?

God's desire

What might God's desire be for this area in your life?

While in this, what might this look like to receive His love toward. you?

Disordered desires...tempt us to suck things into ourselves, and result in the diminishment of the desired object.

Ordered desires expand us without diminishing the other.

They draw us into creative relationship with what lies beyond ourselves without tempting us to try to possess it.

-Margaret Silf, *Inner Compass*

RELEASE TO RECEIVE

Release disorder to re-attach to God

Take a moment in prayer to let go
Of any disordered attachment
in order to re-attach to God...
Trusting He'll help you to rightly attach
to that connection once again

Don't let the world around you squeeze you into its own mold,

But let God re-mold your minds from within...

Fix your attention on God. You'll be changed from the inside out...

God brings the best out of you, develops well-formed maturity in you.

-Romans 12:2 (Phi & MSG)

RELEASE TO RECEIVE

Now take a moment to re-invite God Into that area of desire

- **God created *your desires*,** He is perfectly able to enter into them.

- **Consider inviting God into the desires** that He Himself created in You.

- What would it be like to **share this desire WITH Him?** To walk this out with Him?

- What would it be like in this area **to desire TOGETHER?** What is His heart for this?

WHAT DO YOU DREAM OF?

Pause and share with God about Your dreams...

What did you dream-for early in life?

What dreams haven't worked like you thought?

What are you desiring now?

What is it like to dream again?

Ask God, what are His dreams for you?

What does He desire?

What was He dreaming
when He thought of you?

JOURNAL HERE

JOURNAL HERE

THE PULLEY

When God at first made man,
Having a glass of blessings standing by,
"Let us," said he, "pour on him all we can.
Let the world's riches, which dispersèd lie,
Contract into a span."

So strength first made a way;
Then beauty flowed, then wisdom, honour, pleasure.
When almost all was out, God made a stay,
Perceiving that, alone of all his treasure,
Rest in the bottom lay.

"For if I should," said he,
"Bestow this jewel also on my creature,
He would adore my gifts instead of me,
And rest in Nature, not the God of Nature;
So both should losers be.

"Yet let him keep the rest,
But keep them with repining restlessness;
Let him be rich and weary, that at least,
If goodness lead him not, yet weariness
May toss him to my breast."

a poem by George Herbert

ASK

The purpose of this Christian life is that our hearts might be restored and set free.

JOHN ELDREDGE

Soaking In
SCRIPTURE

Take a breath.

Then read these Scriptures below.

Ask God to open your ears to His Holy Spirit,

Let the words wash over you once.

Then read it again.

Practice receiving these words as...

God's word to you.

SCRIPTURE

Psalm 139:13-18

For You formed my inward parts;
You wove me in my mother's womb.
I will give thanks to You,
for I am fearfully and wonderfully made;

Wonderful are Your works,
And my soul knows it very well.
My frame was not hidden from You,
When I was made in secret,
And skillfully wrought
 in the depths of the earth;
Your eyes have seen
 my unformed substance;

And in Your book were all written
The days that were ordained for me,
When as yet there was not one of them.
How precious also are
Your thoughts to me, O God!
How vast is the sum of them! If I should count
them, they would outnumber the sand.
When I awake, I am still with You.

JOURNAL HERE

SCRIPTURE

Psalm 36:7-9

How precious is
Your lovingkindness, O God!

And the children of men take refuge in
the shadow of Your wings.

They drink their fill
of the abundance
of Your house;

And You give them
to drink of the river
of Your delights.

For with You is the fountain of life;
In Your light we see light.

REFLECTION

What did I learn about myself in this last section?

What did I learn about you, God, in this last section?

If someone were going through a similar season as me, I would share this with them:

DISCERNING GOD'S VOICE

DISCERNING GOD'S VOICE

Have you ever heard the voice of God? Some say it's impossible. Others claim it too readily. Yet, in the Bible, God often speaks to His people. Not only does He speak, but He expects His people to listen like their lives depend on it. A.W. Tozer says it like this:

"In the beginning was the Word...a word is a medium by which thoughts are expressed, and the application of the term to the eternal Son (John 1.1) leads us to believe that self-expression is inherent in the Godhead, that God is forever seeking to speak Himself out to HIs creation. The whole Bible supports this idea. God is speaking. Not God spoke, but *God is speaking.*"

Just like a child longs to hear the voice of their parent, to learn how to live, to hear the truth, to find care, affirmation, and guidance—so our souls long to hear the voice of our Father.

Although, many things compete with our attention to God—that is where our conversational relationship with God can be so crucial. Done well, it accelerates discernment. But even Jesus faced temptation in the wilderness. So we too must prepare to hear God's voice.

Let's take a moment to review how God has already been speaking. To remember *how* He speaks to Christians, and to us personally. Then ask Him to speak to us during our times with Him.

JOURNAL HERE

WAYS GOD SPEAKS...

Underline and note the ways God Speaks in the Bible

And the Lord came and called as before, "Samuel! Samuel! And Samuel replied, "Speak, your servant is listening."

1 Samuel 3:10

And the word of the Lord came to me, saying, "What do you see, Jeremiah?" And I said, "I see a branch of an [b]almond tree." ..."You have seen well,

Jeremiah 1:11-12

As Elijah stood there, the Lord passed by...But the Lord was not in the wind...the earthquake...the fire...after, there was the sound of a gentle whisper. When Elijah heard it, he wrapped his face in his cloak and went out and stood at the entrance of the cave.

1 Kings 19:11-13

We entered the house of Philip the evangelist...this man had four virgin daughters who were prophetesses.... a prophet named Agabus came down from Judea. And he came to us... and said, "This is what the Holy Spirit says...

Acts 21:8-11

They were all together in one place. And suddenly a noise like a violent rushing wind came from heaven, and it filled the whole house where they were sitting. And tongues that looked like fire appeared to them, distributing themselves, and a tongue rested on each one of them. And they were all filled with the Holy Spirit and began to speak with different tongues, as the Spirit was giving them the ability to speak out.

John 17:24

An angel of the Lord appeared to him in a dream. "Joseph, son of David," the angel said, "do not be afraid to take Mary as your wife. For the child within her was conceived by the Holy Spirit.

Matthew 1:20

Now it came about in the thirtieth year, on the fifth day of the fourth month, while I was by the river Chebar among the exiles, the heavens were opened and I saw visions of God.

Ezekiel 1:1

What other ways can you think of? Nature? Scripture? People? Music? Circumstances? What else?

JOURNAL HERE

LISTENING TO HIS VOICE:

Write down one situation or moment where you heard God most clearly:*

if unsure about hearing God's voice, skip forward two pages

What was it like to hear that from Him?

____
____
____
____
____

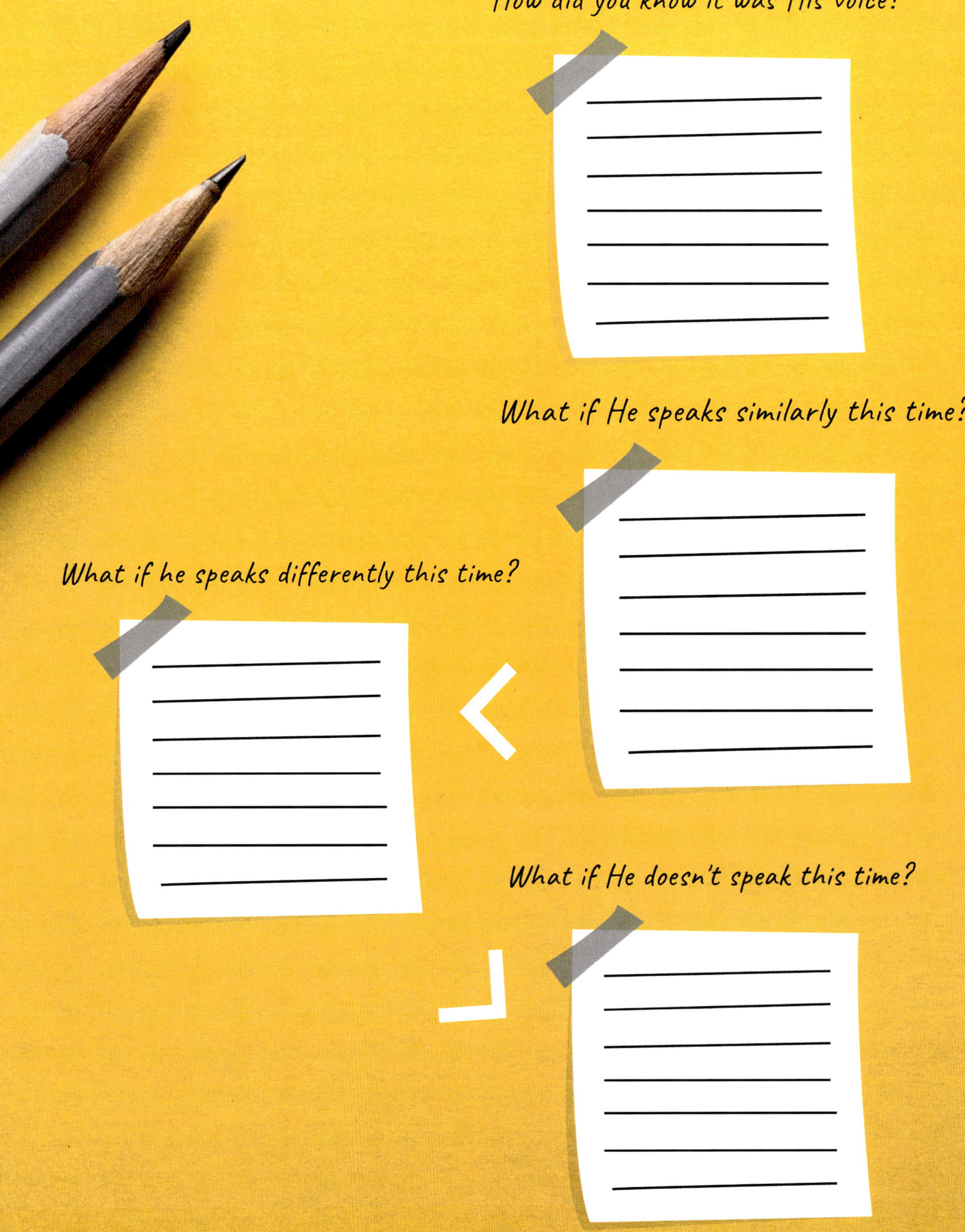
CONSIDER:
How did you know it was His voice?
What if He speaks similarly this time?
What if he speaks differently this time?
What if He doesn't speak this time?

JOURNAL HERE

STRUGGLING TO HEAR GOD?

Draw a picture or write a poem showing God what it feels like to not hear Him

BRAINSTORM THREE THINGS

What might God be doing in this silence?

GOD'S VOICE

BIBLE

CREATIVITY

COMMUNITY

CELEBRATION

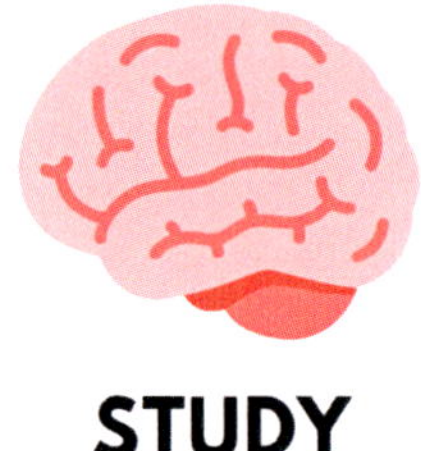

STUDY

NATURE

SERVING

PRAYER

OTHER:___________

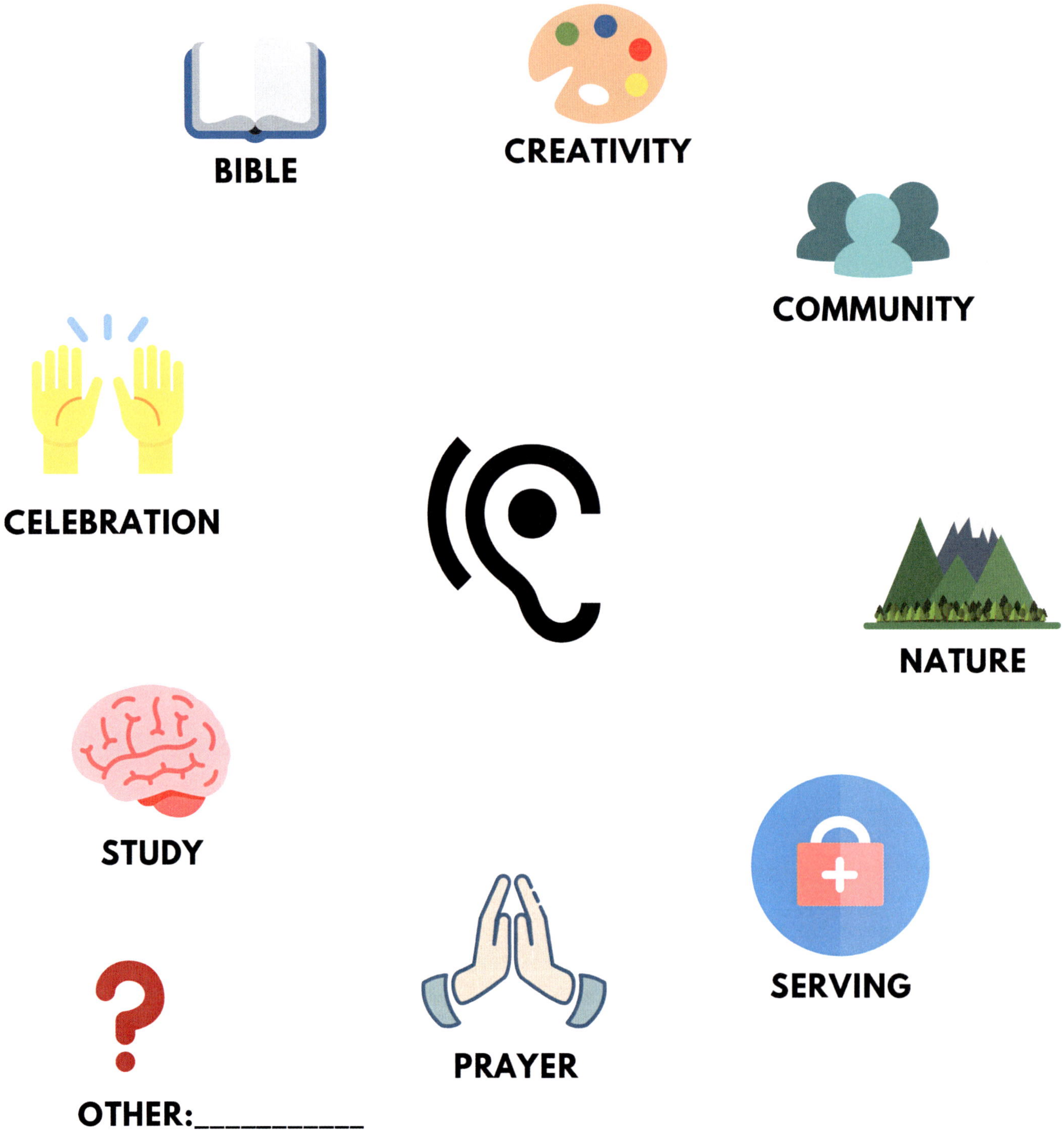

HAVE YOU TOLD HIM

What you would like to hear?

I prayed to **My God** for help *He* heard me from His *Sanctuary* my cry to Him **reached His ears.**

- Psalm 18:6

JOURNAL HERE

OTHER VOICES

What voices compete for your attention?

OTHERS

YOURSELF

THE ENEMY

Write down how these voices might affect your time with the Lord.

JOURNAL HERE

WHO AM I BELIEVING?

God doesn't only say what we *want*
Him to say. His Spirit also trains
us to listen for the *tone* and *character* of His voice.

He will never say anything that contradicts His Character
in the Bible and His perfect love for you, but He does speak differently in
different seasons. Plus, He uses a variety of routes to reveal Himself. What
ways have you noticed Him speaking to you in different seasons?

TRY THIS!

Think of someone you know who seems to know God's voice really well, and ask them what God "sounds" like. Ask them to pray for your time with God too!

A MOMENT TO REFLECT

The Business of Becoming

soft wisps of steam
rise like a dying fire.
i sip the delicate wonder
of a single moment quiet,
in the early morn
before frenzieddesirescrowdin
asking me not so discreetly
to turn from a warm mug,
to stop thinking private thoughts,
to be hurried, productive,
just like everyone ought to, but i ask,

"whose voice is this who speaks so freely
without greeting or introducing,
interrupting a once private moment
before my cup and the day?"

no one answers.

light mist twirls up as comforting hands
strumming a quiet morning song,
that rises early and floats away
on seas of fog toward an endless dawn,
awakening where faces and voices
no longer beckon away and up, bustle and go;
then and now, i will be as steam drawn
into unseen air, dancing as i grow.

believe me, i would rather be in the business of
     becoming
then trapped in a world of clamoring voices.

Soaking In
SCRIPTURE

Take a breath.

Then read these Scriptures below.

Ask God to open your ears to His Holy Spirit,

Let the words wash over you once.

Then read it again.

Practice receiving these words as...

God's word to you.

SCRIPTURE

John 10:14-16, 27-28

I am the good shepherd;
I know my own sheep,
and they know me,
just as my Father knows me
and I know the Father.
So I sacrifice my life
for the sheep...

They will listen
to my voice,
and there will be
one flock with one shepherd...

I know them, and they follow me.
I give them eternal life...
No one can snatch them away from me,
for my Father has given them to me,
and he is more powerful
than anyone else.

JOURNAL HERE

The Spirit, not content to flit
around on the surface,
dives into the depths of God,
and brings out what God planned all along.
Who ever knows what you're thinking
and planning except you yourself?

The same with God—except
that he not only knows
what he's thinking,
but he lets us in on it.
God offers a full report
on the gifts of life
and salvation that
he is giving us.

Spirit can be known only by spirit—
God's Spirit and our spirits
in open communion.
Spiritually alive,
we have access to everything
God's Spirit is doing...

REFLECTION

What did I learn about myself in this last section?

What did I learn about you, God, in this last section?

If someone were going through a similar season as me, I would share this with them:

- SECTION IV -
INVITATION INTO TRUST

INVITATION INTO TRUST

Doubt is a common experience for those who've walked with Jesus. Amid our past, present, and perceived-futures, are scattered disappointments, struggles, and sins that can affect our relationship with God and others. Our authenticity can begin an honest conversation about struggle, pain, and brokenness that is convicting, but sometimes overwhelming. Where do we go when we're struggling to trust God? How can we trust an unseen God if we struggle to trust the person right beside us? Our doubt dealt with apart from God can be debilitating to faith. But doubt *realigned* can bring comfort, renewal, and intimacy. The famous "Hall of Faith" in the book of Hebrews says,

"Now faith is the assurance of things hoped for, the conviction of things not seen. For by it the men of old gained approval. By faith we understand that the worlds were prepared by the Word of God, so that what is seen was not made out of things which are visible," (Hebrew 11.1-2).

So often we place value on *what is seen*; our circumstances, our histories, our failures or successes, and unconsciously sacrifice our relationship with the *Unseen* God, who made us and our world. Sacrifice is always an act of worship. Our first step from disorientation to reorientation will begin with the renewed sacrifice of trusting God again. Trusting Him first with our doubts and all of who we are. Without Him, we sacrifice the *truest reality* of our circumstances.

The Greek word *aletheia* can mean both truth and *reality*. Jesus used this word when he said "Know the *truth* and the *Truth* will set you free." Can you imagine what Jesus's reality looked like? He always saw the world through the eyes of His Father. What do you think that was like for Him to see the prostitutes, tax collectors, roman soldiers, disciples, and pharisees? Were these people worth dying for?

Even Jesus, the wounded Savior, walked through conflict, division, suffering and pain:

"In the days of His flesh, He offered up both prayers and supplications with loud crying and tears to the One able to save Him from death...Although He was a Son, He learned obedience from the things which He suffered. And having been made perfect, He became to all those who obey Him the source of eternal salvation, (Hebrews 5.7-9)."

But Jesus doesn't stop there. He bows His will beneath God's leadership, He begins to offer the most perfect sacrifice, the most wonderful act of worship ever presented to the Father: sacrifice in the midst of unresolved circumstances, sin, hatred, failure, etc.

We will forever be learning the vast implications of this prayer of Jesus: "In the ages to come He might show the surpassing riches of His grace in kindness toward us in Christ Jesus," (Ephesians 2.7).

"TEARS ARE THE ONLY CURE FOR WEEPING...AND YOU MAY HAVE NEED OF THE CURE BEFORE YOU GO FORTH TO FIGHT THE GIANTS."

- GEORGE MACDONALD

What do you think it was like for Jesus to struggle? To feel pain? To walk through suffering? Can you imagine God the Father allowing His beloved Son, Jesus, to endure suffering? "And [Jesus]...fell on His face and prayed, saying, 'My Father, if it is possible, let this cup pass from Me; yet not as I will, but as You will.'" (Matthew 26.39). In Jesus's, worst moments, trust began with an honest heart-cry: "Dad, if it's possible, please take this away!" What an authentic prayer! Jesus felt overwhelmed by the burden God had given Him, and cries out to Him. There's no secret to His prayer life: *just be honest with God*. Our restoration, too, begins with an honest statement, such as, "God, I've forgotten how to trust you, I've been betrayed, disappointed...etc." Just tell Him the weight of the burden.

His one act of perfect worship literally changed all of history and affected all eternity. Jesus rightly connected the longing of His heart to the will of the Father, and by the Spirit brought the power of the good news to full effect on earth. The potency of that one passionate prayer carries us, too, through the cross into the abundant life of the resurrection. If we're longing for restoration, vision, hope, insight, healing, etc., we must approach the Creator again, and ask for His insight. "For he who comes to God must believe that He is and that He is a rewarder of those who seek Him," (Hebrews 11.6). In this section, we begin to articulate our need for God's leadership in our lives. Let this begin a renewed trust in God to lead you moment by moment.

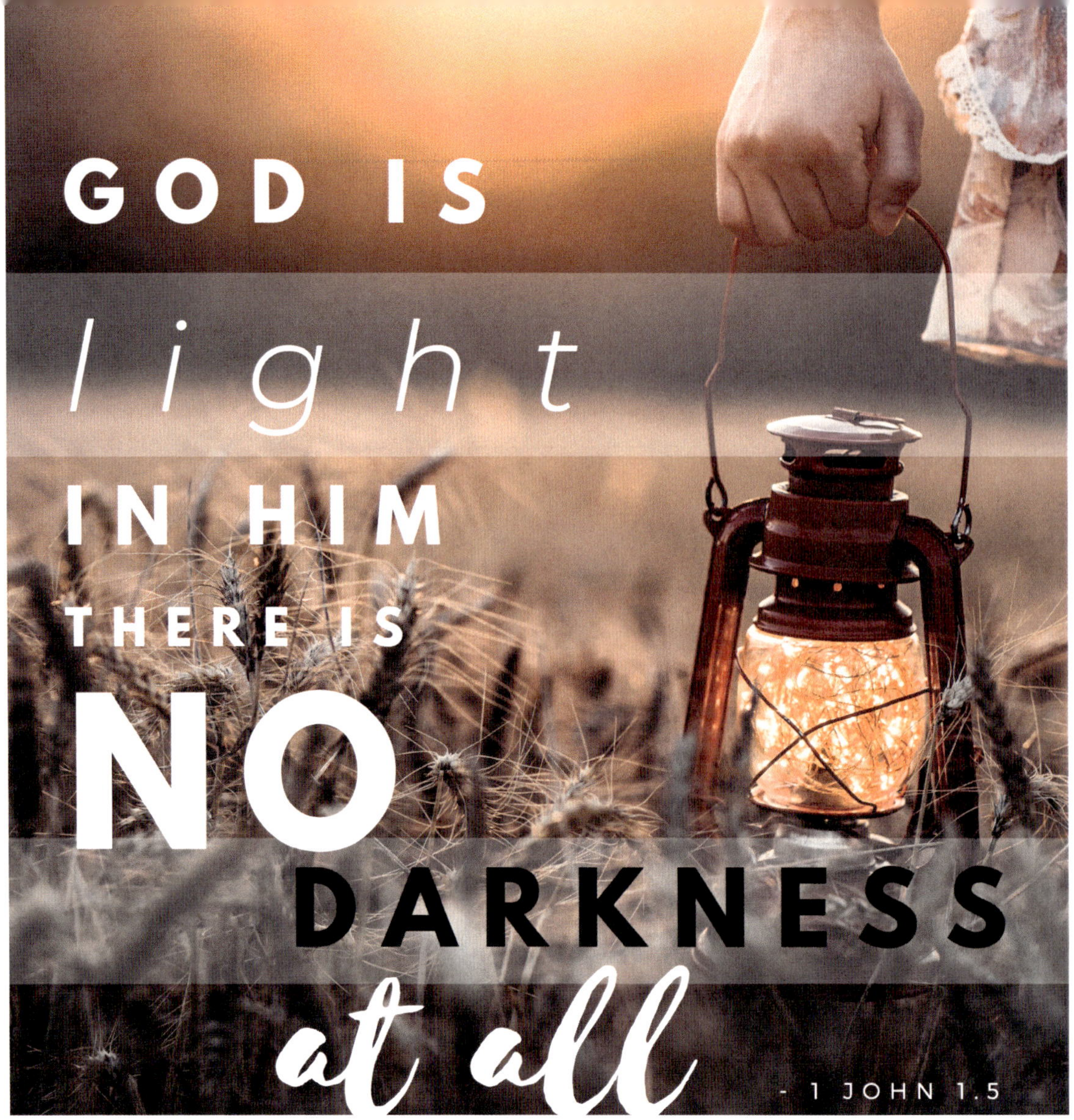

TRUSTING GOD'S LEADING

Over my lifetime, I would rate my ability to trust *God* as:

1   2   3   4   5   6   7   8   9   10

Any season that was harder to trust God?

____
____
____

Over my lifetime, I would rate my ability to trust *others* as:

1   2   3   4   5   6   7   8   9   10

Any season that was harder to trust others?

____
____
____

HISTORY SPEAKS

Let's create a timeline of influence

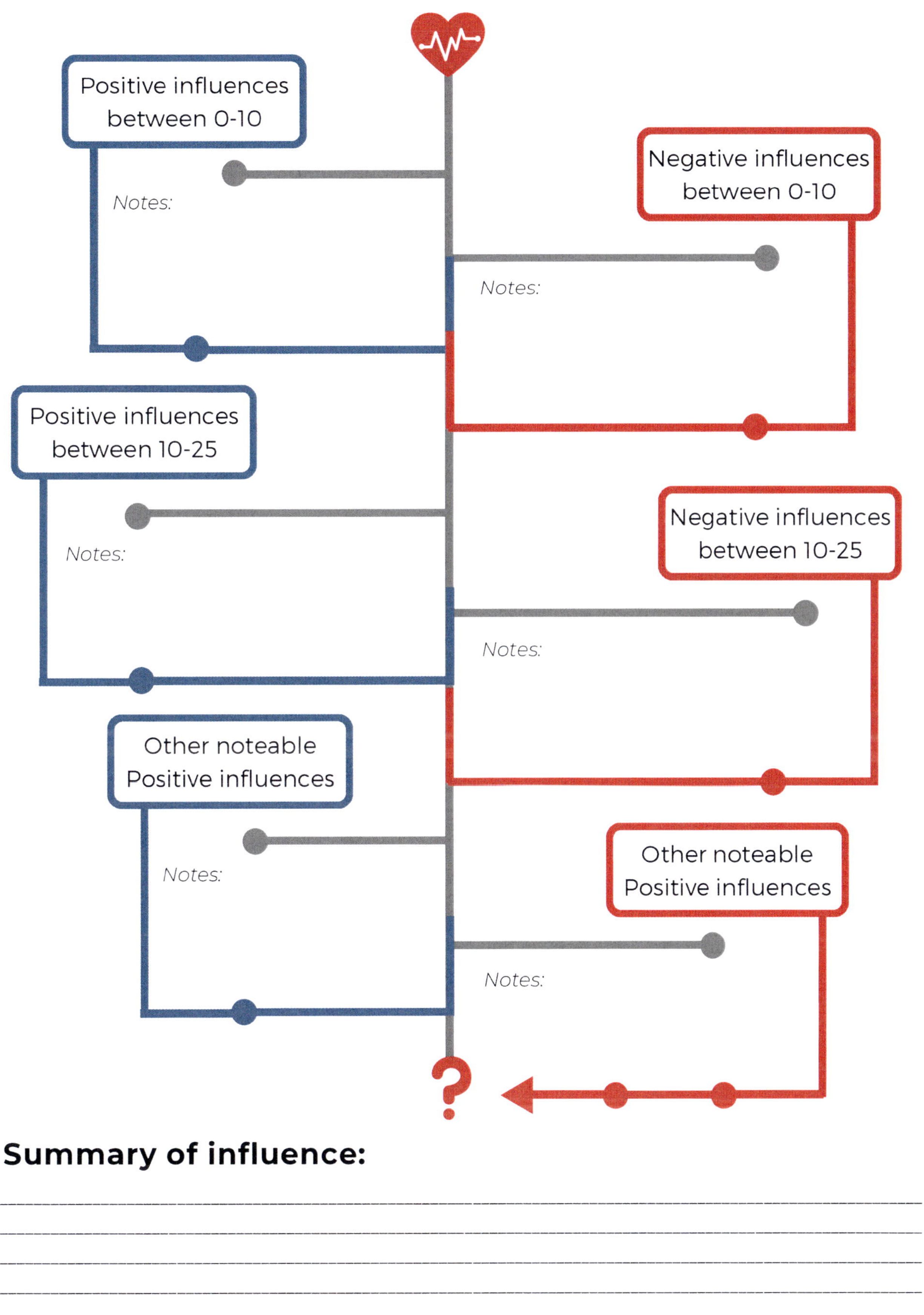

Summary of influence:
____
____
____
____
____

JOURNAL HERE

REINFORCEMENT

Write examples of what the positive leader said or did.

Then write examples of what the negative leader said or did.

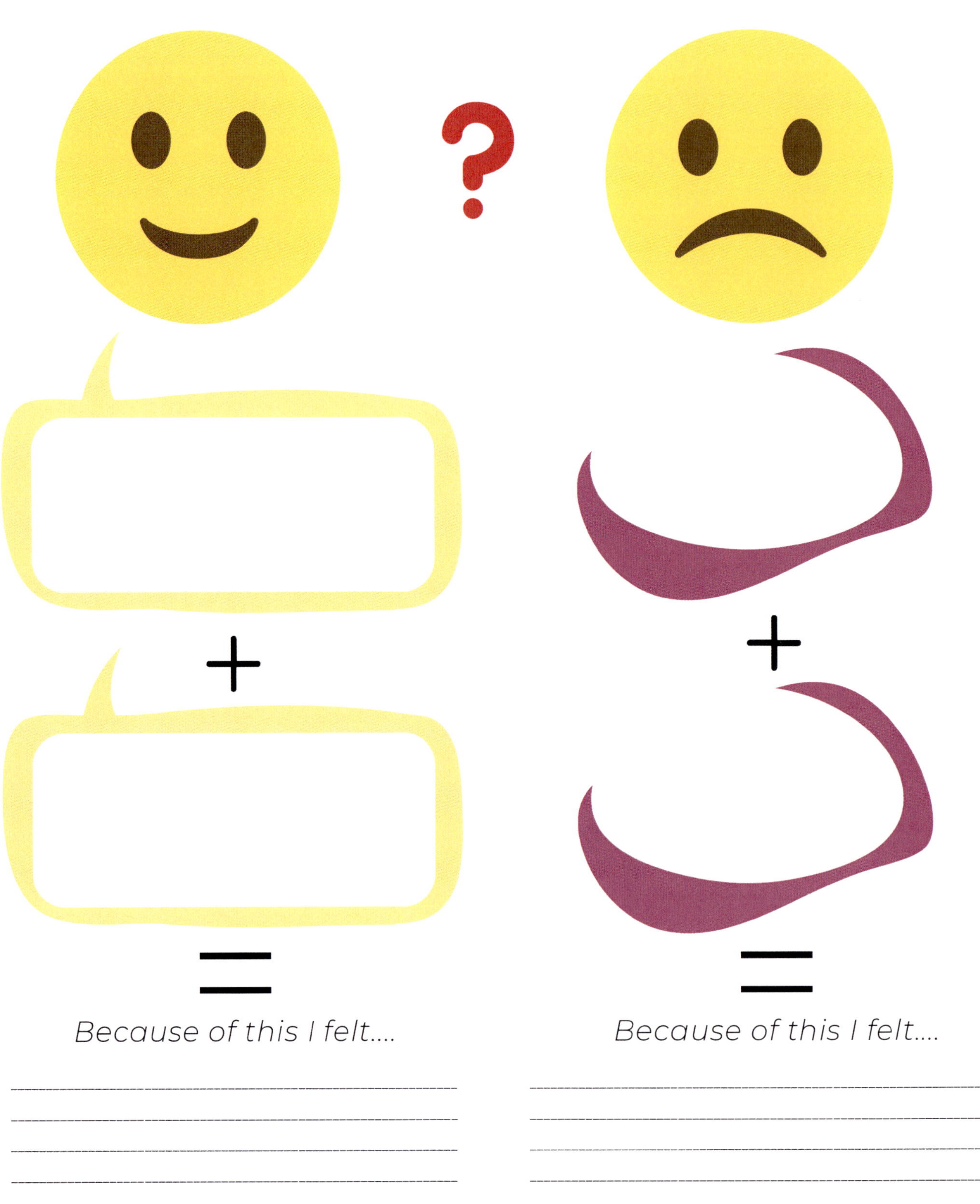

Because of this I felt....

Because of this I felt....

THAT REMINDS ME...

I FEEL LIKE...

How do those words make you feel?

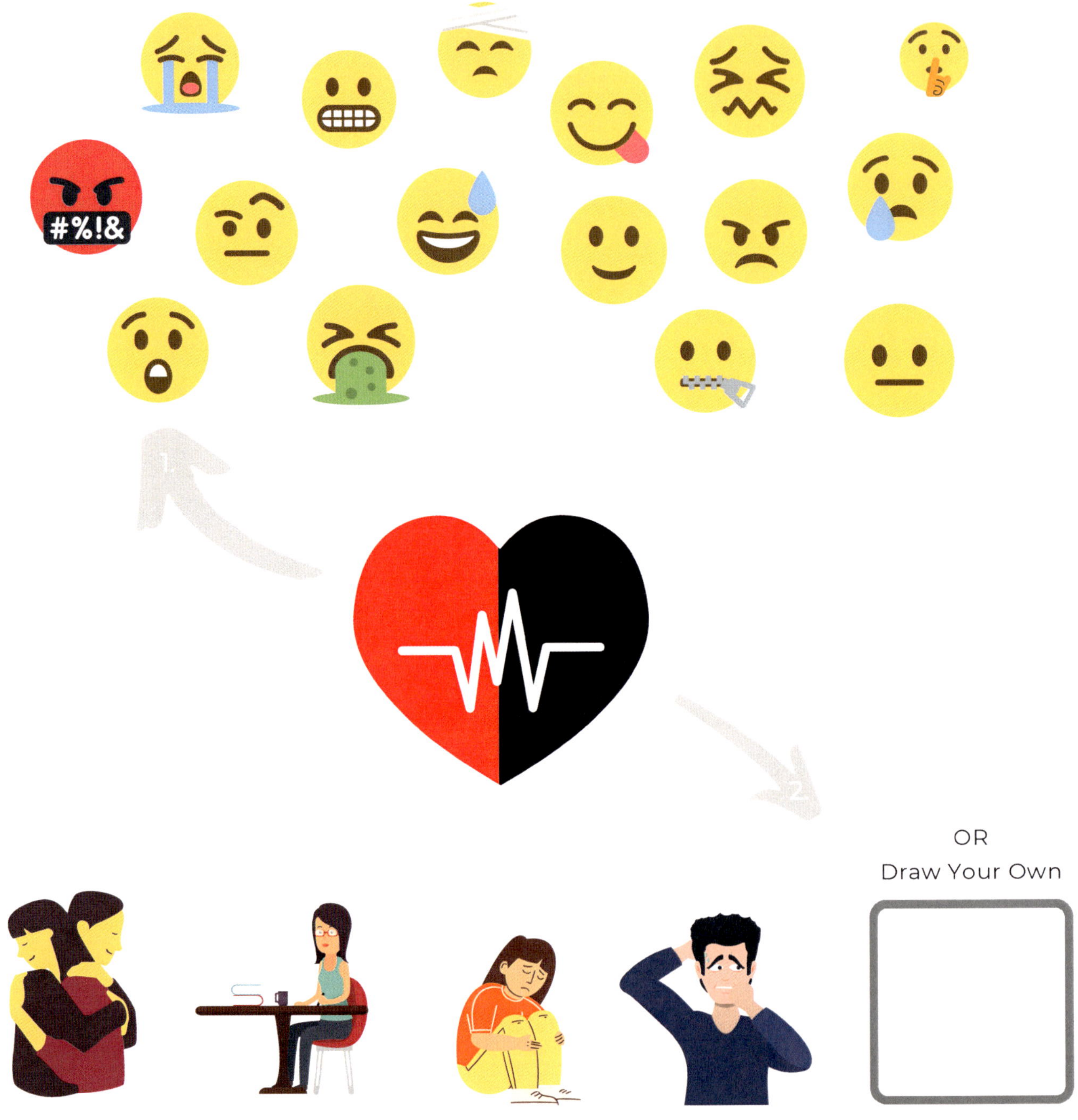

DID YOU KNOW?

You carry those emotions as memories with you?

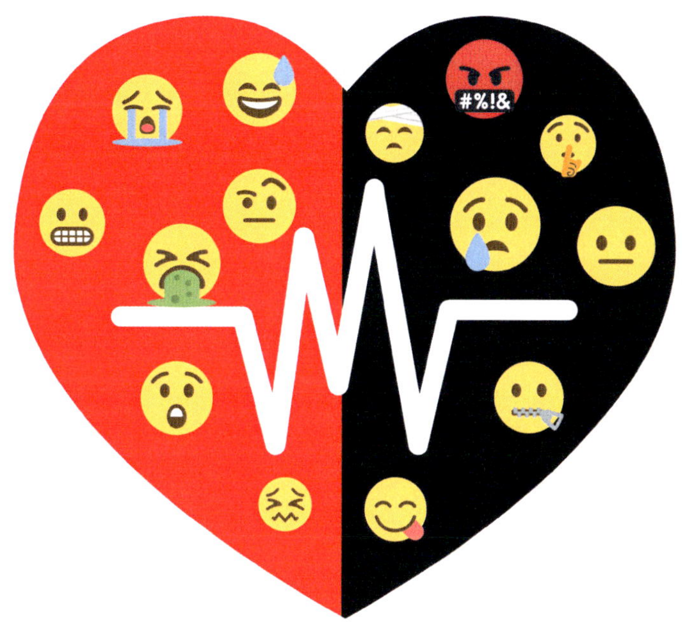

And when an ordinary person or God speaks or acts
it affects those emotions too?

HOW DO YOU THINK

This affects your time with the Lord?

____
____
____
____
____

JOURNAL HERE

SELF-TALK

Jot down some examples of internal "self-talk"

Self-Talk

EX: "I am terrible at spending time with God..."
EX: "God just doesn't speak to me..."

CONNECT TO CLARIFY

Practice turning "Self-talk" into "God-talk"

CLOSE CONVERSATION

Developing honest conversation with God

"God-talk

- "God, I'm struggling"
- "God, I don't know the next step"
- "God, I keep messing up."
- "God, I'm so full of fear"
- "God________________
- "God________________

God's Word

- "Child, I came *for* the sick."
- "Child, nothing can separate us."
- "Child, I dwell with the broken."
- "Child, I call you My beloved."
- "Child, ________________
- "Child, ________________

HOLD THESE BEFORE GOD

Bring your rewritten sentences before God.
Let them soak in the quiet for a few minutes.

This is what I'm noticing after the quiet:

WRITE YOUR LAMENT

Use this structure below to write your own Psalm

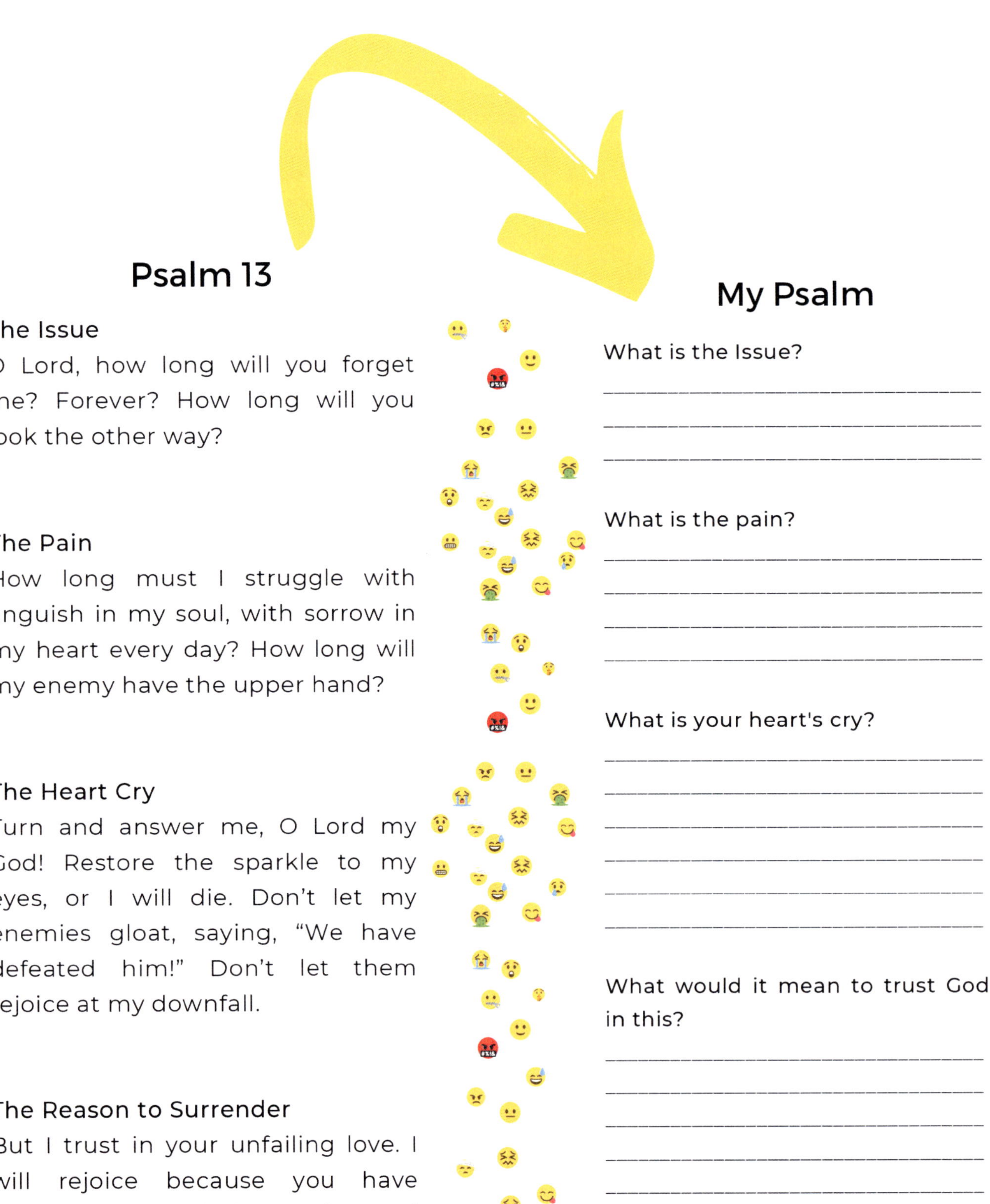

Psalm 13

The Issue
O Lord, how long will you forget me? Forever? How long will you look the other way?

The Pain
How long must I struggle with anguish in my soul, with sorrow in my heart every day? How long will my enemy have the upper hand?

The Heart Cry
Turn and answer me, O Lord my God! Restore the sparkle to my eyes, or I will die. Don't let my enemies gloat, saying, "We have defeated him!" Don't let them rejoice at my downfall.

The Reason to Surrender
But I trust in your unfailing love. I will rejoice because you have rescued me. I will sing to the Lord because He is good to me.

My Psalm

What is the Issue?
____
____
____

What is the pain?
____
____
____
____

What is your heart's cry?
____
____
____
____
____
____

What would it mean to trust God in this?
____
____
____
____

JOURNAL HERE

IN GETHSEMANE

Now, bring that lament to Jesus...

Consider, He also suffered...

He lamented too...

Asking His Father...

To take this cup from Him...

Luke 22:42

Sit with Him for a moment...

What stirs as you're with Him here?

"My soul is crushed with grief to the point of death. Stay here and keep watch with Me."...He was in such agony of spirit that His sweat fell to the ground like great drops of blood.

Mt 26:36 & Lk 22:44

BRING IT TO THE CROSS

Now bring that lament to the Cross...

It's only Jesus's cross that can deal with the...

largest emotions

heaviest disappointments

worst voilations

deepest offenses

He carried it ALL on His Cross...

Jesus cast out unclean spirits with a word...

and healed all who were ill...

This was to fulfill what was spoken through Isaiah the prophet...

"He Himself took our infirmities and carried away our diseases."

Matthew 8:16-17

What did He CARRY FOR YOU?

What do YOU NEED FROM HIM?

A MOMENT WITH GOD

Everyone who thirsts,
come to the waters;

And you who have no money
come, buy and eat.

Come, buy wine and milk
Without money and without cost.

Why do you spend money
for what is not bread,

And your wages
for what does not satisfy?

**Listen carefully to Me,
and eat what is good,**

**Delight yourself
in abundance.**

**Incline your ear
and come to Me.**

Listen, that you may live.

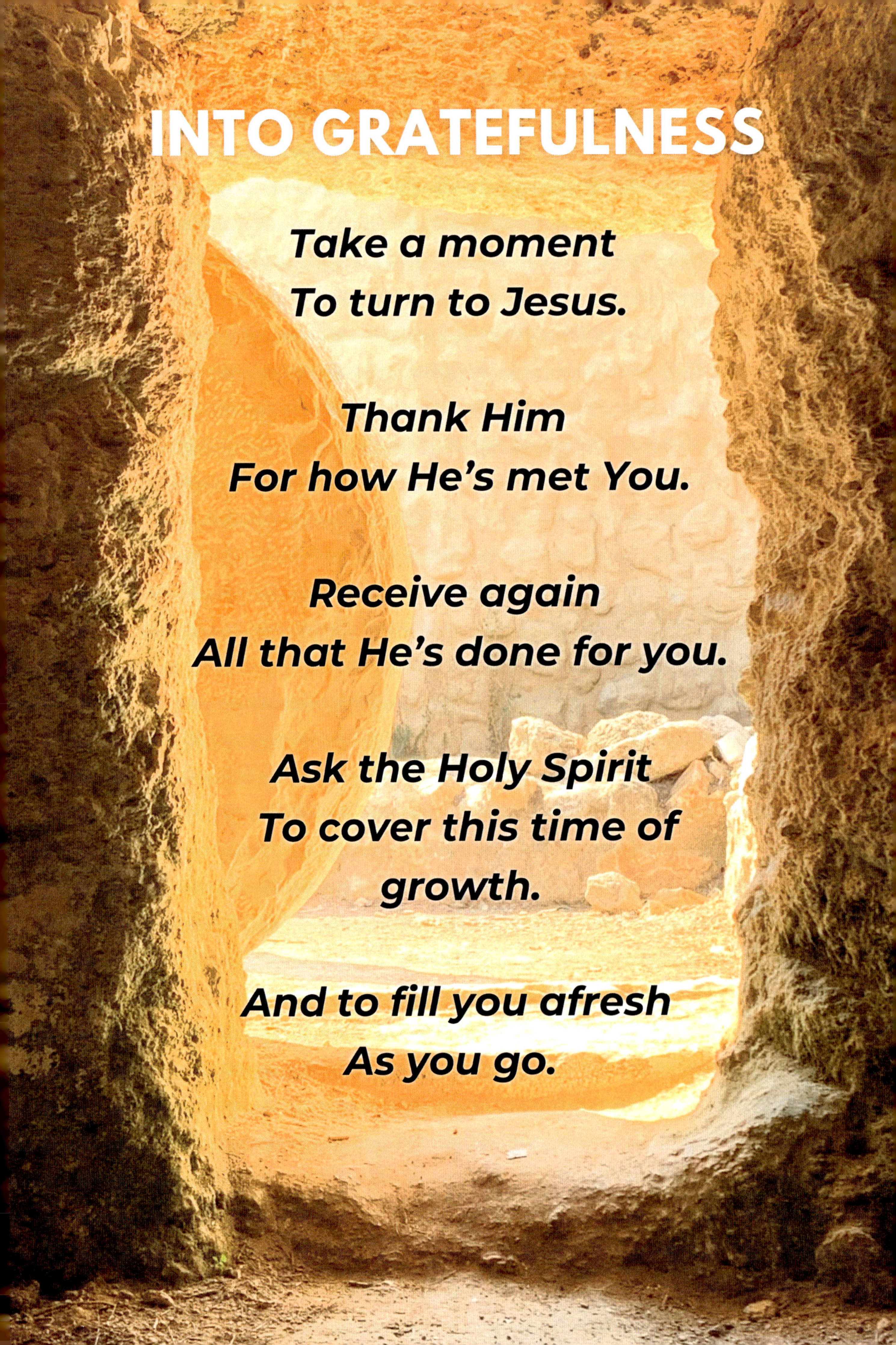

INTO GRATEFULNESS

Take a moment
To turn to Jesus.

Thank Him
For how He's met You.

Receive again
All that He's done for you.

Ask the Holy Spirit
To cover this time of
growth.

And to fill you afresh
As you go.

JOURNAL HERE

SCRIPTURE

**Your Word is a lamp to my feet
And a light to my path.**

- PSALM 119:105

Take a breath.

Then read these Scriptures below.

Ask God to open your ears to His Holy Spirit,

Let the words wash over you once.

Then read it again.

Practice receiving these words as...

God's word to you.

2 Corinthians 7:8-11

I see that [I] caused you sorrow,
though only for a while...
I now rejoice, *not* that you were
made sorrowful, but that you
were made sorrowful to the point
of repentance;
for you
were made
sorrowful
according to the
will of God, so that
you might not suffer
loss in anything
through us.

For the sorrow that is according
to the will of God produces
a repentance without regret,
leading to salvation, but the sorrow
of the world produces death.
For behold what earnestness this very thing,
this godly sorrow, has produced in you...

SCRIPTURE

All around us we observe
a pregnant creation. The difficult times
of pain throughout the world are simply
birth pangs. But it's not only around us;
it's within us. The Spirit of God is arousing us within.

These sterile and barren bodies
of ours are yearning for
full deliverance. That is why
waiting does not diminish us,
any more than waiting
diminishes a
pregnant mother.
We are enlarged in
the waiting. We, of course,
don't see what is enlarging us.
But the longer we wait, the larger
we become, and the more joyful our expectancy.

Meanwhile, the moment we get tired in the waiting,
God's Spirit is right alongside helping us along.
If we don't know how or what to pray,
it doesn't matter.
He does our praying in and for us,
making prayer out of our wordless sighs, our aching
groans...we can be so sure that every detail in our lives
of love for God is worked into something good.

REFLECTION

What did I learn about myself in this last section?

What did I learn about you, God, in this last section?

If someone were going through a similar season as me, I would share this with them:

Appendix
LINGER LONGER

A Guide for Your Retreat

If you haven't already, partner with a Spiritual Director, a trained listener
ready to offer one-on-one care and guidance

We'd love to connect you with someone to help sift through the content
that has arisen on your journey and beyond

Contact us at Soul-Care.com

LINGER LONGER

Reflection for your Retreat

As your journey through this devotional comes to a close, you may be thinking "What now?" What does it mean to continue developing this conversation with God?

What does it look like to stay with this dynamic relationship with God and maybe go even deeper?

Actually, you've already begun that process.

You've already spent time reflecting and inviting God into the reality of where you are currently, which is so foundational. Now, the next step is synthesizing and retelling the story of your journey with God. Considering with Him, what you've noticed? What has your experience of God been like? What has He been nudging and forming in you?

Use this space below to reflect on your journaling and devotional time. We suggest making an intentional retreat space where you can *linger longer* with God. This will aid in the integration of all you have walked through. It will also be a training ground for developing times like this with Jesus in the future.

This can be done in a variety of ways, depending on your season of life. It may be set aside time for a retreat at a cabin or beach house. Or it may be sectioning off one or two half-days at home. Or it may be joining a facilitated experience with a Spiritual Director, Pastor, or Group Leader. Whatever way you choose, utilize the questions and framework below during your time, and soak in the work God is already actively doing in your story.

Take pauses between the pages. Jot down Scriptures. Listen for insights. Soak in what God has done and *is doing*. These things that surfaced are meant to be a launching pad and training ground for what daily deeper conversation can be like as you walk in an intimate relationship with God. Take some time to sense what areas He is highlighting to you and inviting you to remember and continue to explore.

Linger with Him. Let Him lead. Lean into His already-active work in you.

Linger to Remember

*You shall **remember** all the ways in which the Lord your God has led you in the wilderness...*

For the Lord your God is bringing you into a good land, a land of brooks of water, of fountains and springs, flowing forth in valleys and hills; a land of wheat and barley, of vines and fig trees and pomegranates, a land of olive oil and honey;

A land where you will eat food without scarcity, in which you will not lack anything; a land whose stones are iron, and out of whose hills you can dig copper. When you have eaten and are satisfied, you shall bless the Lord your God for the good land which He has given you.

Deuteronomy 8:2-10

Section I - A Deeper Dialogue

Use this for the first hour/day of your retreat

Revisit this section, and consider the questions below

What did I notice about you, God? *Talk with Him further about this.*

____

____

What did I notice about myself? *Share what you learned with Him.*

____

____

Note 2-3 Scriptures that were significant for you from this section. What about these stood out to you?

____

____

____

What are 1 or 2 themes that you notice in those Scriptures? Do others come to mind that complement or nuance these?

____

____

____

What might shift or move in those Scriptures that lead you into prayer? Praise? Lament? *Use your time to express these to God. Spend time listening for Him too.*

____

____

____

As you review the section, notice the parts of your heart or mind that seem to draw you away from the Lord. What was disordered, disoriented, or detracting from your relationship with Him?

____

____

____

Notice any patterns or themes in your heart and mind. Do you notice internal reactions or judgments to your own process? *Share these with God who gave His Son to forgive and heal you.* Invite Him into all that comes up when you think about these.

____

____

____

What if the pattern or theme you notice could be an area that reminds you to come to Jesus? What if you could share that pattern with Him?

____
____
____

How might these patterns connect you more deeply with Him?

____
____
____

Lastly, consider one of these patterns/themes to intentionally invite God into during your time with Him. What would it be like to receive His healing presence in this area?

____
____
____

What might it be like to experience His acceptance and love for you, and to begin a journey toward freedom (2 Corinthians 3:17)?

____
____
____

As you review the sections, consider any gifts or strengths of yours that stand out. What do you notice about your reaction to noting your gifts/strengths?

____
____
____

Consider spending time thanking God for these aspects of your personality. What would it look like to express this aspect of you more fully? Praise Him that you really are fearfully and wonderfully made (Psalm 139). How might these gifts/strengths connect you more deeply with Him?

____

____

____

Lastly, consider a gifts/strength to delight in during this time with the Lord. What would it be like to explore this gift/strength with Him? To experience *His* delight? And to delight *with* Him too?

____

____

____

Prayer Prompt: *(use at the end of each of the following sections)*

Dear Jesus, whether I feel it or not, I know You're in the midst of my heart and mind. Your Holy Spirit is working in the deep places of my life. I open more of me to Your Presence now, especially as I reflect on our times together. It has been a gift to be with You in this season.

Lord, I ask for Your guidance as I lean into this time of retreat with You. With all that we've journeyed through, come, shape, and fill the space. I don't just want more content, but I want You.

Thank you for making me, for shaping me. I ask that even the hard things would be spaces in my life in which You re-create. and make something beautiful. You know what You're about...

And I ask that all that I am would be moved, softened, known, and touched by You, the One who loves me, accepts me, and gave life, and wants to fill me with His abundance.

Come, Lord Jesus, have Your way. *Amen.*

Use this for the second hour/day of your retreat

Revisit this section, and consider the questions below

What did I notice about you, God? *Talk with Him further about this.*

____

____

What did I notice about myself? *Share what you learned with Him.*

____

____

Note 2-3 Scriptures that were significant for you from this section. What about these stood out to you?

____

____

____

What are 1 or 2 themes that you notice in those Scriptures? Do others come to mind that complement or nuance these?

____

____

____

What might shift or move in those Scriptures that lead you into prayer? Praise? Lament? *Use your time to express these to God. Spend time listening for Him too.*

____

____

____

As you review the section, notice the parts of your heart or mind that seem to draw you away from the Lord. What was disordered, disoriented, or detracting from your relationship with Him?

____

____

____

Notice any patterns or themes in your heart and mind. Do you notice internal reactions or judgments to your own process? Share these with God who gave His Son to forgive and heal you. Invite Him into all that comes up when you think about these.

____

____

____

What if the pattern or theme you notice could be an area that reminds you to come to Jesus? What if you could share that pattern with Him?

____

____

____

How might these patterns connect you more deeply with Him?

____

____

____

Lastly, consider one of these patterns/themes to intentionally invite God into during your time with Him. What would it be like to receive His healing presence in this area?

____

____

____

What might it be like to experience His acceptance and love for you, and to begin a journey toward freedom (2 Corinthians 3:17)?

____

____

____

As you review the sections, consider any gifts or strengths of yours that stand out. What do you notice about your reaction to noting your gifts/strengths?

____

____

____

Consider spending time thanking God for these aspects of your personality. What would it look like to express this aspect of you more fully? Praise Him that you really are fearfully and wonderfully made (Psalm 139). How might these gifts/strengths connect you more deeply with Him?

____

____

____

Lastly, consider a gifts/strength to delight in during this time with the Lord. What would it be like to explore this gift/strength with Him? To experience His delight? And to delight with Him too?

____

____

____

Take a moment, Reread Prayer Prompt

Section III - Discerning God's Voice

Use this for the third hour/day of your retreat

Revisit this section, and consider the questions below

What did I notice about you, God? *Talk with Him further about this.*

____

____

____

What did I notice about myself? *Share what you learned with Him.*

____

____

____

Note 2-3 Scriptures that were significant for you from this section. What about these stood out to you?

____

____

____

What are 1 or 2 themes that you notice in those Scriptures? Do others come to mind that complement or nuance these?

____

____

____

What might shift or move in those Scriptures that lead you into prayer? Praise? Lament? *Use your time to express these to God. Spend time listening for Him too.*

____

____

____

As you review the section, notice the parts of your heart or mind that seem to draw you away from the Lord. What was disordered, disoriented, or detracting from your relationship with Him?

____

____

____

Notice any patterns or themes in your heart and mind. Do you notice internal reactions or judgments to your own process? Share these with God who gave His Son to forgive and heal you. Invite Him into all that comes up when you think about these.

____

____

____

What if the pattern or theme you notice could be an area that reminds you to come to Jesus? What if you could share that pattern with Him?

____

____

____

How might these patterns connect you more deeply with Him?

____

____

____

Lastly, consider one of these patterns/themes to intentionally invite God into during your time with Him. What would it be like to receive His healing presence in this area?

____

____

____

What might it be like to experience His acceptance and love for you, and to begin a journey toward freedom (2 Corinthians 3:17)?

____

____

____

As you review the sections, consider any gifts or strengths of yours that stand out. What do you notice about your reaction to noting your gifts/strengths?

____

____

____

Consider spending time thanking God for these aspects of your personality. What would it look like to express this aspect of you more fully? Praise Him that you really are fearfully and wonderfully made (Psalm 139). How might these gifts/strengths connect you more deeply with Him?

____

____

____

Lastly, consider a gifts/strength to delight in during this time with the Lord. What would it be like to explore this gift/strength with Him? To experience His delight? And to delight with Him too?

____

____

____

Take a moment, Reread Prayer Prompt

Section IV - Invitation into Trust

Use this for the fourth hour/day of your retreat

Revisit this section, and consider the questions below

What did I notice about you, God? *Talk with Him further about this.*

____

____

What did I notice about myself? *Share what you learned with Him.*

____

____

Note 2-3 Scriptures that were significant for you from this section. What about these stood out to you?

____

____

____

What are 1 or 2 themes that you notice in those Scriptures? Do others come to mind that complement or nuance these?

____

____

____

What might shift or move in those Scriptures that lead you into prayer? Praise? Lament? *Use your time to express these to God. Spend time listening for Him too.*

____

____

____

As you review the section, notice the parts of your heart or mind that seem to draw you away from the Lord. What was disordered, disoriented, or detracting from your relationship with Him?

____

____

____

Notice any patterns or themes in your heart and mind. Do you notice internal reactions or judgments to your own process? Share these with God who gave His Son to forgive and heal you. Invite Him into all that comes up when you think about these.

____

____

____

What if the pattern or theme you notice could be an area that reminds you to come to Jesus? What if you could share that pattern with Him?

____

____

____

How might these patterns connect you more deeply with Him?

____

____

____

Lastly, consider one of these patterns/themes to intentionally invite God into during your time with Him. What would it be like to receive His healing presence in this area?

____

____

____

What might it be like to experience His acceptance and love for you, and to begin a journey toward freedom (2 Corinthians 3:17)?

____

____

____

As you review the sections, consider any gifts or strengths of yours that stand out. What do you notice about your reaction to noting your gifts/strengths?

____

____

____

Consider spending time thanking God for these aspects of your personality. What would it look like to express this aspect of you more fully? Praise Him that you really are fearfully and wonderfully made (Psalm 139). How might these gifts/strengths connect you more deeply with Him?

____

____

____

Lastly, consider a gifts/strength to delight in during this time with the Lord. What would it be like to explore this gift/strength with Him? To experience His delight? And to delight with Him too?

____

____

____

Take a moment, Reread Prayer Prompt

JOURNAL HERE

CONTINUE IN WHAT YOU HAVE LEARNED
- 2 TIMOTHY 3:14

**For more content
resources and guidance**

Visit us at Soul-Care.com

find rest for your soul

Made in the USA
Monee, IL
20 February 2025